D0811117

Mastering the Public Spotlight

Mastering the Public Spotlight

by Arnold Zenker

DODD, MEAD & COMPANY
New York

Copyright © 1983 by Arnold Zenker
All rights reserved
No part of this book may be reproduced in any form
without permission in writing from the publisher

Published by Dodd, Mead & Company
79 Madison Avenue, New York, N.Y. 10016
Distributed in Canada by
McClelland and Stewart Limited, Toronto

Manufactured in the United States of America
Designed by Denise Schiff

First Edition

Library of Congress Cataloging in Publication Data

Zenker, Arnold.
  Mastering the public spotlight.

  Includes index.
  1. Public speaking. I. Title.
PN4121.Z44 1983 808.5′1 83–11530
ISBN 0–396–08233–5

To my parents,
  whose love and support
    have forever enriched my life

Acknowledgments

A respected colleague once told me that a professional communicator sweats and strains long hours *backstage* so that thirty minutes *onstage* can appear easy and effortless. To the degree the writing of this book appears easy and effortless, foremost credit goes to Debra J. Saunders. As editor of first resort, she ferociously attacked each draft, always striving for changes and additions to make it better. Her wise input is incorporated into every page of the finished product. My thanks, also, to John Kaufmann for troubleshooting when I needed it, to Dr. Suzanne Swope for reading and approving the technical information about voice and articulation, and to my editor at Dodd, Mead, Jerry Gross, for invaluable direction and control. Finally, warm appreciation and affection are due my wife, Barbara, and my daughter, Jennifer, for showing remarkable patience and good humor while I griped and groaned my way through this project.

ARNOLD ZENKER
BOSTON
MARCH 1983

Contents

PART FOUR:

ON THE TUBE

PART FIVE:

FROM THE ROSTRUM

PART ONE

Perspectives

1 Beginnings: Who Am I? Why Did I Write This Book? What Can I Offer You?

It usually happens this way: You are sitting comfortably in your office on a Friday afternoon, looking forward to a relaxing summer weekend. The vice-president of Finance strides through the door. "Jones," he says, "I'm scheduled to address the Society of Security Analysts in New York on Monday and I'm not going to make it. You fill in for me."

Or this way: An emergency exists. A drainpipe at the plant has burst and thousands of gallons of polluted water are discharging onto the surrounding landscape. As chief engineer, you're up to your elbows trying to bring the situation under control. An assistant runs in shouting, "Chief, the Channel 3 investigative team has arrived and they want to interview you."

Or maybe this way: A farewell dinner has been scheduled for a loyal colleague who is retiring after thirty-five years on the job. As his closest friend, you are chosen to serve as master of ceremonies.

Tough situations, but not uncommon ones. Eventually, the responsibility of standing up and speaking out to a watchful audience confronts everyone. Even the shyest are vulnerable. As Robert Frost wrote, ". . . all who hide too well away/Must speak and tell us where they are." Some people welcome these challenges; a great many more face them with emotions close to terror.

If you fall into the latter category, you are the victim of a self-imposed malady that limits your personal and professional potential unnecessarily. I say that with conviction—a conviction earned after more than a decade of helping people like you *master the pubic spotlight*. Furthermore, I know you can be trained to become a communicator of professional caliber. Accomplishing that is my business.

My firm's clientele includes some of the nation's major corporations, industry trade associations, professions, universities, and government agencies. From the oil fields of Texas to the ski slopes of British Columbia, from farmers to funeral directors, from hospital administrators to politicians, we have provided training in the techniques of making more effective public appearances.

These appearances can run the gamut from being interviewed on the television evening news to facing an angry group of stockholders or consumers, from testifying before a government regulatory committee or local school board to speaking to a foreign trade group or social club. Sometimes it simply involves making a presentation to a company's executive committee.

During the ten years my firm has been in operation, our business has boomed. I have never attempted to calculate in a scientific manner the exact number of trainees who have been schooled in our methods, but taking into account presentations before large groups at conventions and meetings, workshops and individual counseling, that number may approach fifty thousand. And certainly we are not alone in providing this service.

There are dozens of firms prospering by helping people improve their communication skills. *The Directory of Personal Image Consultants* lists fifty-four companies specializing in speech/public appearance training. Others offer wardrobe analysis, personal promotion and motivation, goal-setting and career development —all variations on the same theme. There is clearly a huge demand, and the reasons for it are easy to determine.

First, people want to feel comfortable when addressing an audience. For personal and career reasons, they want to command attention and get a message across. That attitude is demonstrated in our workshops when I ask participants why they are attending. Here are some sample answers:

"I desperately want to be a better communicator. My job calls for that talent. I lack it, and the lack is hurting my career advancement."

"I am sick and tired of feeling faint when my name is called to make a report. How do I gain confidence?"

"I look out at bored faces whenever I speak and it's demoralizing. There must be a better way."

"As a child, I hated being on the stage. As an adult, I hate it. I wish I didn't."

Second, we all recognize that in contemporary society the written word is yielding to oral communication as the primary method of getting across information. Few people today engage in extended correspondence with family and friends; instead, they settle for sending a cute greeting card. Generations hence, it is unlikely that readers will find many books entitled *The Collected Letters of . . .*

In business, memos and reports are still abundant, but the telephone and meetings are widely utilized as a quicker, more interactive way of sharing data. According to a survey by the consulting firm Booz Allen & Hamilton, about 46 percent of an executive's time is spent in conference. Efficient use of the telephone and meetings depends upon oral-presentation skills.

The future promises to accelerate the trend away from writing and toward the spoken word. The "video society" has blossomed. A wired nation is no longer a dream; it's a reality. Miniaturization has brought the cost of cameras and recorders down into the range of most budgets, and these items are becoming fixtures in our homes and offices. Children create their own programs; corporations construct internal systems for use in product introduction and employee training. A Ford may or may not be in your future, but you can be certain that telecasting is.

Whatever the job title, whatever the occupation, whatever the field or industry, competence in—more than that, mastery of—public communication skills will be essential. I assume you agree. Otherwise, you wouldn't have this book in your hands. But since many of the theories and concepts I present here may seem radical to the layperson, I should establish my credentials. Let me quickly summarize how I became a "communications consultant."

Right Time—Right Place!

The spring of 1973 found me in Boston, hosting a daily, hour-long television interview and variety show on WCVB-TV, Channel 5. One afternoon, an official of a local company called me, introduced himself, then quickly got to the point. "Look," he said, "our people are getting slaughtered by the television press and we just don't know how to handle it. Can you put together some kind of workshop to train them in techniques of dealing effectively with the media?"

Train executives how to appear on television? The proposal struck me as curious. As an interviewer, I had experienced my share of inept guests from the business and professional communities. That they were not so much inept as untutored simply had never occurred to me, although, of course, it should have. Few executives arrive in positions of power with much experience behind a microphone or in front of a camera. As a utility executive once said to me, "I'm just an accountant. What the hell do I know about show business?"

Yet in the early 1970s, big business had become the object of intense scrutiny by consumer groups and government regulatory agencies. With their arsenal of television equipment, reporters were peering into corporate boardrooms, searching for someone in authority to explain why this river was polluted or that line of toys injured children or this group of employees alleged racial or sex discrimination. No one in those boardrooms wanted to reply. "No comment!" became a corporate catchphrase. Correspondents retaliated by aiming a lens at the closed company door. "We tried to interview Mr.——, but he refused to speak." That implication of guilt had a devastating impact.

Finally it dawned on corporate and bureaucratic America that if the private-enterprise side of the story were ever to be heard, their own people were going to have to tell it. But their own people simply didn't know how. Confronting a communications debacle, organizations under attack naturally went hunting for help. That explained the motivation underlying the call I received from the local company. As it turned out, other media professionals were receiving similar calls for aid from executives of other firms and industries in distress.

When I look back at the program I conducted for my first client, I blush at its primitiveness. Still, the participants liked it and found it valuable. I liked it too. In many respects the work made full use of a store of knowledge I had acquired.

From the time I became an announcer on the University of Pennsylvania's radio station, I have been hooked on the broadcasting business. The old expression is that when it comes to careers many are called, but few are chosen. I was lucky enough to be both. Throughout my years in college and law school I moonlighted as a disc jockey and newsman at a local radio station. When I got my LL.B degree I never even seriously considered joining a law firm. Instead, I went to the American Broadcasting Company in New York as a general-management type assigned to labor relations. In 1965, I switched over to CBS News, first in business affairs, later in documentary program administration. Then followed six years as a television and radio news and public affairs personality in Baltimore and Boston.

The radical shift from management to on-camera work came about as a freakish byproduct of the first and only strike ever called against the three major networks by the national performers' union in its fifty-year history.

And Now Substituting for Walter Cronkite

On February 27, 1967, while manager of News Programming administration at CBS, I sat in a staff meeting half listening to a network radio executive list which management, nonunion personnel had been tapped to fill in on the air if the contract dispute with AFTRA (American Federation of Television and Radio Artists) was not settled. One slot, a midafternoon newscast, remained open. Bill Leonard, my boss and vice-president of Programming, said, "Zenker's done a lot of radio. Why don't you let him handle it?" I thought little of the exchange at the time since I was certain there would be no strike.

Later that day, Leonard summoned me to his office. Bill, whose name may be familiar to you since he subsequently became president of the News Division, informed me, "If they go out tomorrow, you're going to substitute for Benti." (Joseph Benti anchored the "CBS Morning News" from 7:00 to 8:00 A.M.)

"Come on, Bill," I replied, "my background is radio. I've never spent any time on camera."

"Then it's a good time to learn."

That was it. To this day, I don't know what prompted that decision. I do know that, contrary to all logic, AFTRA and the networks broke off bargaining at midnight and the union went on strike. At 4:00 A.M., I waved to the pickets I knew personally as I entered the studio and began rehearsing. (To clear the record, I was not a scab. I had no union affiliation at the time, and management personnel are expected to help out during labor difficulties.)

The producer of the "Morning News" and I were casually acquainted. Years before, while still in law school, I had auditioned to become a weekend anchorman at a TV station in Cleveland where he was news director. He didn't hire me.

"Can you use a teleprompter?" he asked me.

"I don't know. I've never tried. But if I'm going to see the print, I'd better wear my glasses."

My TV debut went surprisingly smoothly. There were no fluffs, stumbles, or embarrassments—a minor triumph for which I gave credit to all those hours spent behind a radio microphone. Looking into a camera seemed just a natural extension.

Feeling pleased, I walked over to Bill Leonard's office. He was on the phone with Frank Stanton, CBS president. When the call ended, he turned and said, "Get ready to fill in on the 12:25 news telecast—after you do the 11:00 A.M. radio news on the hour. By the way, Stanton thought you were fine."

By midafternoon, a veteran of two TV and two radio network newscasts, I headed for a cab to go home. On the way out, a man stopped me in the hallway and asked for my home phone number.

Incredible as it sounds, I never made the connection as to why Ernie Leiser, producer of the "CBS Evening News with Walter Cronkite," wanted my number. Two hours later, awakened out of a deep nap by the phone's harsh clanging, two and two finally added up. "Come back," said Ernie Leiser, "you're going to substitute for Cronkite."

I could write a separate book on my two weeks filling in for the most famous anchorman in America. Sixteen years later, people ask me what it was like. I understand the phenomenon. It is the age-old tale of the understudy who substitutes for the star and receives critical raves. Who can resist such a fable?

In my case, the public first reacted with incredulity. As *Time* magazine put it, "This is the *CBS Evening News* with Arnold Zenker substituting for Walter Cronkite. *Arnold Zenker?*" As days passed and I survived the perilous situation, the incredulity turned to affection and complimentary notices. By the second week, columnists were busy speculating about my future as a broadcaster. I recognized the fundamental reason for all the hoopla.

There were many on-air substitutes during that strike, but only one person who occupied Walter Cronkite's throne. I was, and am, a competent broadcasting talent, and I had put in thousands of hours before the microphone by the time network duty called. Press coverage carefully overlooked this experience since it made better copy to paint me as a total innocent. But had I surfaced in a less visible location, the impact would have been nil. Starring on the "CBS Evening News" turned me into a temporary celebrity. When the strike ended after thirteen days, Walter Cronkite opened his first broadcast with the line, "Good evening. This is Walter Cronkite sitting in for Arnold Zenker." That gracious statement became the quote of the day in the *New York Times.*

While my taste of glory had been heady, it created the need for some serious decision making. Walter Cronkite, after all, was still Walter Cronkite. Who, now, was Arnold Zenker? Did I stay in management or opt for an on-camera career? Offers were coming in. CBS News was equally perplexed. As a senior colleague put it, "They've created a monster and now they don't know what to do with him." For nearly six months I vacillated, unable to make up my mind. Then a chance occurrence made the decision clear.

A documentary producer, needling me one day, joked, "You know, Arnold, you've got a great future behind you." That did it. I knew then and there I had to get out.

In September 1967, accompanied by another burst of publicity, I joined Westinghouse Broadcasting's WBZ-TV in Boston as an anchorman-reporter. I worked the next six years in a variety of on-air roles. Then in 1973, I received that fateful telephone call that put me into the public appearance consultant business.

Right Time—Right Profession!

Initially, I gave little thought to the idea of communication training as a full-time venture. Consulting was a sideline that offered additional stimulation and income. Two fortuitous events dramatically changed my casual outlook.

First, my television program was canceled, a victim of poor ratings. In the lingo of the industry, I was suddenly "at liberty." Although I quickly picked up a daily talk show on a local radio station, I had lots of free time to concentrate on building the consulting operation. Almost concurrently, the Arab oil embargo of 1973 created an instant, giant market for communication consultants.

Those of us who lived through it remember how anarchy reigned as motorists literally fought and killed for precious gallons of gasoline. Pessimists predicted the end of our industrial empire. Citizens called for the nationalization of the oil business. Congress created the Energy Department, which exploded seemingly overnight into a $14-billion bureaucracy. Oil companies, public utilities, or any enterprise remotely connected to the problem of keeping us fueled and warm, had to account to the public for their activities. They sought help in getting that message across. In one six-month period, from July through December 1974, I earned more money working with energy firms than I had with all other clients prior to that time. The pace never slackened . . . and for me an avocation became both a full-time occupation and a fascinating way of life.

The challenges of my career are as diverse as the people I work with. One week may provide the stimulation of prepping a corporate chief executive officer for a battlefield confrontation with "60 Minutes," while the next offers the quiet gratification of assisting a superbly qualified physician to overcome his inability to communicate with patients.

As a so-called "image doctor" or "image maker," I have been both applauded and damned. The criticism arises from the misconception that people in my trade are charlatans who encourage deception by preaching illusions at the expense of truth. We do preach *illusion,* and I am certain you will understand why as you read on. I am also certain that you will share my conclusion that the teaching methods we pioneered deserve a larger audience than I can ever reach on a person-to-person basis. A book—this book—resulted.

There is no point in pretending that this text will ever take the place of hands-on instruction, but it does offer a few extra benefits. In the course of our normal training session, I rarely get a chance to provide the perspectives and philosophies that are contained here. Yet they are the foundation that, in effect, defines the difference between a routinely talented musician and a creative virtuoso.

I have labored hard to structure this material as if you were an actual "client," seeking and deserving a sophisticated training approach aimed at making you a virtuoso communicator. My goal is to pass along to you the insights known and acted upon by professionals in this field so that, whether you have to appear before a technical group, local service club, or village board meeting, you will be judged as having *mastered the public spotlight.* Now, let's begin.

2 You-the Client

If you are agreeable to the idea of becoming a client, then you might as well experience what a client goes through when we first meet.

There are methods and formulas unique to every business. When you enter an attorney's office to seek advice about a divorce, the counselor automatically will hand you a questionnaire seeking information about you and your spouse, your children, and your family assets. Before the lawyer can provide you with specific advice, a general profile of your situation is necessary.

When I meet a client the first time, I make a similar audit. I attempt to size up, through the use of both gentle questioning and intuition, what the client is really all about. The following are some questions I might ask myself. How would you respond about yourself?

1.   How effective as a communicator is the person sitting across from me?

2. What weaknesses (such as monotone voice, inexpressive face, etc.) are immediately obvious?

3. By contrast, what are the inherent strengths on display (dynamic personality, poise, etc.)?

4. What life or business crisis has brought on this surge of interest in communication? As a practical matter, most people shun training until it is absolutely necessary. Why is the client seeking my help so urgently?

5. What does the client consider reasonably achievable goals? How professional does he or she want to become?

6. In my judgment, how many of these goals are realistic? Has the client under or overestimated his or her potential? (Curiously, my experience is that most people expect too little of themselves.)

Notice that emphasis on the *person,* not on procedures, is the key to my training approach. I am not a public speaking coach who gets forty dollars an hour and earns every dollar of it. We charge thousands of dollars a day for our counseling. What justifies the fee differential? The sophistication and flexibility of our techniques, and the magnitude of our goal—to package a superbly *professional communicator.*

Public speaking coaches learn a series of rules about communication while in school and then repeat them verbatim as teachers. Sometimes the rules are archaic and senseless. When I thumb through academic texts in this field, I shudder in disbelief over the content.

Just to cite two examples: it is useful advice, I suppose, to keep your hands away from your pockets when addressing an audience, since jangling change is disconcerting. But suppose you empty the change before beginning and keep your inserted hand still? Anything wrong with that? Of course not. To viewers, what is jarring are random, unstructured hand and body movements. But stillness doesn't attract undue attention and can't hurt you.

Similarly, there is a modicum of truth to the bromide that draping your body over a lectern while speaking is unattractive. But if you treat the lectern as a dramatic prop, then you can thump it, hide behind it, place an elbow on it, or do anything else so long as the choreography enhances your message.

Innocence and inexperience once caused me to be entrapped by an arbitrary rule about dealing with audiences. At age sixteen, I took my first speaking course from a woman who had capitalized on a small acting talent to become the reigning czarina of my high school dramatic department. The lady is memorable to me mainly for her carrot-colored hair, a pince-nez that perpetually slipped down her nose, and for giving me my first opportunity as an actor. She had one other trait: her steadfast insistence on the "laws of public speaking." In her eyes they were no less important—or unchangeable—than the commandments delivered from the mount.

Two weeks into the semester, I had to make my first attempt at giving a talk in front of the class. Trembling, I took my best shot and held on for the required five minutes. I do not recall what I said or even what my topic was. But, over twenty-five years later, the finale remains etched in my memory. As I came to the conclusion of my speech, I thanked those assembled for their attention.

"Stop!" shrieked the instructor. "Stop this instant! You never thank an audience! *Never!* It should be grateful for the privilege of listening to you!"

My face flushed brighter than the lady's hair. I didn't argue or debate the point. Humiliated by the snickering of classmates, I sat down as quickly as possible. And, for years afterward, I would choke at even the thought of muttering those forbidden words— *thank you*—when concluding a presentation. Until sometime, somewhere, sanity gained the upper hand, and I gingerly tried the words again. The audience didn't turn on me. No lightning bolt struck from heaven. It was even a nice touch. I liked it. I had learned that if I wanted to say thank you, or anything else for that matter, I could do it, because, once onstage, I called the shots. So much for rules.

As a consultant, my focus is on shaping a person's style. I am not a psychiatrist committed to comprehending and curing neuroses. I'm not concerned with the inner person known only to family and

God. Instead, it is the exterior *image* with which an audience comes into contact that is my province. As you will learn, image and effective communication are symbiotic and inextricably linked.

Let me illustrate how my system works by introducing you to a client. In Chapter 1, I mentioned having worked with a physician whose practice suffered from his inadequate communication skills. His story is an interesting one. The doctor and I came into contact because of a call from his wife. She had read an article about me in *Patient Care,* a medical journal, and wondered whether our techniques might be of benefit to her spouse.

As she described him to me on the telephone, he was a highly devoted practitioner who felt an enormous commitment to quality health care. But, in his mind, he had translated that concern into a need to have long visits with every patient, answering every question, responding to every complaint. The result? Probably one of the few medical practices in the United States on the verge of running in the red.

On meeting him personally, my first reaction to the doctor was surprise at how little talent he had for small talk. The "hellos" and "how are yous" that lubricate introductions were simply lacking. His core of shyness manifested itself in a chill exterior. It was as if a plexiglass shield separated us.

After chatting for a while, I asked the doctor to play a brief game with me. He was to assume the two of us have met at a medical conference. The point of first contact in the morning is the refreshment table in the back of the room, laden with sweet cakes and pots of coffee and tea. As we fill our cups, the conversation is trivial. Where are you from? How was the weather when you left? Good plane trip? Perhaps a brief discussion about the leading news item of the morning. Chances are we barely glance at each other during this period. Instead, we concentrate on our hands, sugaring our beverage, selecting a doughnut, gathering a napkin. Finally, the preliminaries over, we actually face each other and begin to extend the range of our discussion. I ask what brings the doctor to the conference. In turn he speculates about how the program will develop over the next several days.

The entire interaction, from coffee line to the moment we drift apart in search of other conversations, has lasted no more than three minutes. I asked the doctor, "If at that instant a policeman materialized, pad in hand, and asked me to describe you, Doctor, how would I respond?" The doctor's face went blank. Silence pervaded the room for about thirty seconds. Then he responded, "How much can you know about me from such a superficial contact?" The answer was, of course, a great deal.

When any of us meet someone new, we immediately draw conclusions, accurate or inaccurate, about age, social status, ethnic background, educational level, and affluence. It is these snap judgments that influence our decision on whether to pay attention to the new acquaintance or walk away in search of a more fulfilling contact. It is important to keep in mind that the identical process takes place when a speaker meets an audience. There the group is cataloging impressions. How it ultimately responds to the speaker's message and to the information offered depends in substantial part upon its perceptions of the speaker as a person.

My video technician had already set up the equipment and I proceeded to tape a conversation with the doctor in which I played patient. When we replayed the simulated visit, the doctor seemed shocked. The man he saw on the screen had little to do with his own self-image as a physician. The man on the screen entered the make-believe examining room with his back to the patient, sat down quickly, pulled out a notebook, and began taking a history. Never did he engage in any prolonged eye contact or allow himself the chitchat that might have made me, the patient, feel welcome.

Furthermore, the language in which the doctor sought information from me was highly technical and verbose. Much of the time it required rephrasing before I understood what he was asking. Finally, the doctor did not know how to say, "Goodbye, this session is over." Instead, as long as I raised imaginary complaints or asked off-the-wall questions, he attempted to deal with them.

"Doctor," I said finally, "is that scene indicative of good medical practice? Does it benefit either the patient or your pocketbook? Can a way be found to accomplish both goals more effectively?"

In broaching these issues, I intentionally created a major obstacle. It is exceedingly difficult and painful for us to admit that the way in which others perceive our personality and effectiveness may differ substantially and negatively from our own carefully developed self-image. This reluctance is exaggerated when the subject is personally and professionally successful. Indeed, the higher the position people attain in life, the less likely they are to hear about their annoying traits. Few patients would dream of asking an intimidating physician to "stop rambling and get on with your opinion for heaven's sake"; few underlings have the courage to suggest to the chairman of the board that he is a bore.

The typical, though often unspoken, reaction to my critical evaluation is, "Look at me. I am president of this . . . a director of that . . . a respected member of my community. How dare you suggest I present myself poorly?" The doctor responded predictably when he said, "This has been an unfair situation. I am uncomfortable with you and the camera and the lights. In my own office, with my own staff, treating my own patients, I am a different person."

Admittedly, the environment of an initial training session is intimidating and can produce a distorted picture, but not as distorted as the doctor so desperately wanted to believe. Stress and unfamiliarity may account for a 15-percent error factor, but 85 percent of a person's image displayed on the screen will be an accurate reproduction of the presence they actually project.

In order to move forward, I had to convince the doctor that the tale told by the videotape is accurate, so I suggested a second trial run. The exercise would be easier for him, I noted, since we had already acted the roles, and he knew the questions I would ask. I urged him to relax on the next go-around and to utilize every opportunity to display himself most positively.

To the doctor's consternation, the playback of the second drill revealed only modest improvement in his interpersonal communication skills. He still came across as distant, wooden, and uncertain. He still tended to use fifty words when fifteen would have sufficed. He still found it difficult to end the encounter.

I could have lectured the doctor incessantly about his weaknesses, and he would have remained stubbornly skeptical. Confronted with another taped example of the ineffectual way he had handled the hypothetical office situation, his resistance to my observations crumbled.

The doctor's experience is shared by most of my clients, and turns out to be a version of the "good news–bad news" jokes. The "bad news" is that the unfavorable image of themselves they see on tape is actually the image *others* perceive, and it is often a humiliating lesson. Worse, it is a useless lesson if they simply walk away proclaiming, "I hate the way I look." The fundamental question every client—*you*—must ask is: What elements of this image I now project diminish my ability to send the message I want to send? Do I suffer from lack of facial expression or voice variety, convoluted grammar, appearance of arrogance, poor choice of clothing, or the wart on my nose?

In the doctor's case, the answers were relatively straightforward. He had to learn how to be more forceful with voice projection and body language. He had to carefully choose his words in order to avoid redundancy and rambling. He had to recognize that setting a time limit with a patient is the authority figure's responsibility. He had to make up his mind that practicing good medicine involves more than knowing his stuff; it requires, as well, understanding how to communicate his knowledge.

The "good news" for all clients is that bothersome characteristics that impede successful communication usually can be quickly corrected. Helping people make these changes, after all, is what I get paid for and what this book is all about.

Although most of my clients are interested in improving their appearances on the television screen or at the rostrum, I deliberately chose the physician's case to emphasize my approach and procedures because it enables me to make several basic points.

Public Appearances Cover a Broad Spectrum

To the physician, every visit with a patient constituted a public appearance. And you "make a public appearance" every time you conduct a meeting, teach a class at church, or make a pitch to your boss for a raise. At first it may not seem that way. But if you have to communicate with a person or group of persons in a formalized setting where the outcome is important, your presence and conversation are no longer a casual matter. The techniques we discuss in these pages have application not only to public communication, but to a wide range of interpersonal situations as well.

The "Personal" and the "Public" You Are One

The manner in which the doctor handles his patients, or you your own interpersonal contacts, is only a slightly modified version of the way both of you will treat an audience while making an address, testifying before a committee, or guesting on a television talk show. In other words, the difference, the separation between the *real you* and the *public you* is very narrow. There is a myth that we present a different, a separate personality when facing an audience.

For the most part, that is simply not true. We are one person, and regardless of format or forum, we communicate with only slight variations. If you don't look an acquaintance in the eye when speaking, chances are you don't look an audience in the eye either. If you don't project your voice while at a dinner party, you probably are just as faint at a meeting. If you fidget and fuss while lecturing your teenager, be assured that you most likely appear equally nervous when addressing your staff.

I don't want to overstate this point. Obviously, there are comfortable situations that afford you the opportunity to shine. But though actors change their personalities at will to meet the demands of a role, most people can't make such radical adjustments.

Image and Substance

Finally and most important: How successfully you or the doctor communicate, whether in a one-on-one situation or before a crowd of thousands, depends as much upon the *image* conveyed as the *substance* of the message. In fact, the less the other party (or audience) needs to know about the information you offer, the more the equation swings in favor of *image*. That may shock you. Certainly, the concept runs counter to the commonly held one that oral communication is mainly the delivery of facts and figures.

Convincing the client to appreciate the impact of *image* is, to me, a first and essential step in creating a professional communicator. The next chapter explains why.

3 Images

Around a large table sit a number of monks. The vows of their order demand silence. A bowl of Rice Krispies sits before each monk. Milk is poured on the cereal. Horror of horrors, the cereal begins to chatter—to snap, crackle, and pop. The smiling faces of the monks experiencing the sound of the cereal are wonderful to behold. Praise the Lord! Rice Krispies make a good, noisy, friendly companion at breakfast time.

Forgotten, of course, in the humor of the message, is that the way Rice Krispies sound has little to do with the way they taste. The manufacturer knows this. They also know that the old adages —"sell the sizzle, not the steak," "sell images, not information"— still hold true. Why?

Because obtaining *information* through oral communication is a very difficult process. When we read, we can move forward at our own pace. If we choose, we can reread complex sections. But words, spoken aloud, are like fireworks that explode in the atmosphere for an instant, dazzle with light and color, then disappear. There is no opportunity to rehear them. Once uttered, they are lost. The more words there are, the more words are lost, thus increasing the information gap.

The old adages also remain true because we are incompetent listeners. Survey after survey has shown that of the content offered during a ten-minute oral presentation, only 50 percent is retained. Two days later, 50 percent of that 50 percent has fled from the mind, leaving a net of only 25 percent retention and comprehension. (My own guess is that these figures err on the optimistic side.)

So, when we watch a secretary of state on a television news program hinting at possible military action against another country, the message (shrouded in diplomatic language) often passes us by. Were the program a football game, of course, we would be treated to instant replays of the action. But ideas are not accorded the same respect. We are expected to process complicated information on the first go-around. We can't and we don't.

Instead, what remains in our minds are perhaps a few headlines and the *image* of the person holding centerstage. We remember the image of an overly ambitious Alexander Haig, the former secretary of state, seemingly eager to assume power after Ronald Reagan was shot. We recall the perspiration on his face and the palpable agitation of a personality nearly out of control. That image, not his comments, shaped a national impression of Haig that remained long after Reagan had recovered.

Just look at the importance of *image* in shaping voter decisions during election campaigns. Issues lag far behind impressions in determining victors and losers. The most famous examples of this are the 1960 Kennedy-Nixon television debates. If you were to analyze carefully the audio tape of those debates, you would conclude that Nixon was the sharper candidate, possessing a better grasp of ideas and complexities. But viewers *watch* television, they don't *listen* to it. Visually, Nixon appeared pallid and ill, his unmade-up face swallowed by an oversized collar. The media-wise John Fitzgerald Kennedy, pointed index finger emphasizing his statements, came across as handsome and virile. Overnight, Kennedy became the front-runner in the race, a position he maintained through election day and victory.

A similar *image* problem doomed Gerald Ford when he debated Jimmy Carter in 1976. Here, Ford began with the advantages of incumbency and a public perception of his having done a good job leading the country out of the morass of Watergate. Unfortunately, Ford also carried the burden of being a fumbler, a man who banged his head on helicopter doors and tripped down airplane steps.

During the televised confrontation between the two candidates, Ford blithely described Eastern Europe as free of Soviet domination. The panel of questioners flinched. One reporter, with unusual graciousness, urged clarification, practically pleading with Ford to admit Eastern Europe fell within the sphere of Russian control. Stubbornly, Ford stuck to his guns. It was quite a moment. With a single stroke of his tongue, wrote one satirist, Ford managed to free Poland single-handedly. The following day, the press had a field day with Ford's mistake; the bumbler had stumbled again. Carter waltzed into the presidency.

Ironically, Carter fell prey to the same *image* problems when he squared off against Ronald Reagan in 1980. Whatever his other weaknesses as chief executive, no one ever questioned Carter's intelligence or diligence. But he was up against probably the best political communicator since Franklin D. Roosevelt.

Sure, Carter had facts at his fingertips. But Reagan had something better, a style and demeanor that calmed and reassured an electorate badly in need of a paternal pat on the head. Almost immediately after the first debate, Reagan's stock began rising in the polls. Commentators later indicated that viewers best remembered two specific moments about the dialogues. One came when Carter expressed his deep concern over the risks of nuclear proliferation. He felt so strongly, he said, that he talked it over with daughter Amy. You could almost feel the home audience wince, saying to itself, *"Amy? He talked it over with Amy?"*

The second was when Ronald Reagan, in response to a Carter assertion, good-humoredly waved his hand in the president's direction and, as if exasperated by his adversary's point of view, exclaimed, "There he goes again." Poor Jimmy went. Back home to Plains, Georgia.

Political consultants have long understood such tactics and acted accordingly. They merchandise the candidate, not the candidates' beliefs and positions. They tailor the "package" exactly as if it were designer blue jeans. Aim at a specific market. Paint an attractive *image* in bold, broad strokes. That has become the way to bring home the ballots.

A legitimate philosophical question emerges. Is this concentration on a politician's *image* harmful to our democratic system? Who can intelligently say? There are no quantitative data to support the argument that the presidents we chose before television were any better equipped or more successful than today's creatures of the media. Indeed, if the presidency is a "bully pulpit," as Teddy Roosevelt called it, the competence of a chief executive may be less important than his ability to win and use that pulpit effectively.

On the other hand, common sense should demand that government leaders be more than movie stars. A brilliant actor like George C. Scott, for example, may know how to depict a man of presidential stature. It doesn't follow, however, that he would be worth a damn in conducting public affairs.

I don't have an answer to this dilemma. I do know that technology has changed, once and for all, the way information is disseminated and that *image* now dominates every aspect of our lives. It figures in the cars we buy, the toothpaste with which we brush, the cosmetics we apply, and even the mates we select.

Image plays a major part in the degree of impact that you have, for better or worse, when making a speech, arguing with a local zoning committee, or confronting the home audience via television.

I concede that the degree to which *image* dominates content will vary with the motivation of the listener(s). When I visit my doctor, for example, in search of a diagnosis of an illness, I am highly attuned to content. Whether I have skin cancer or a benign lesion is more on my mind than the *image* of the doctor giving the opinion. Yet even here, the way the doctor *appears* to me in conveying that information has significance. If he or she seems wishy-washy or callous or inattentive, then regardless of the ultimate verdict, I may leave feeling insecure and unsatisfied. Have you ever been given good news by a physician so unconvincingly that you went to another specialist just for reassurance? I certainly have.

But if the doctor-patient relationship is at the high end of the motivated-listener scale, a typical speech to a service club audience is at the other. Chapters of service clubs hold weekly luncheon meetings, each featuring a guest speaker. The attendees know little about the speaker and care even less. Listening is an obligation, to be borne for a fixed period of time. The consolation is that the speaker stops after twenty minutes. How much information do you think such an audience absorbs? Virtually nothing. Perhaps, if the speaker did an especially good job, a few headline-sized ideas may stick. Mostly, though, the members depart with a sense of, a reaction to, the speaker. Was he prepared? Did she seem knowledgeable? Was the experience entertaining? They will take away impressions—*images.*

On television, in live appearances, in interpersonal contacts, it's the *image* of you that *counts!* Is this external *you* any less real than the internal personality you know and cherish? To the contrary. Willard Gaylin, M.D., professor of clinical psychiatry at Columbia University, puts this issue in sharp focus:

> The inside of a man represents another view, not a truer one. A man may not always be what he appears to be, but what he appears to be is always a significant part of what he is. . . . The inner man is fantasy. If it helps you to identify with one, by all means do so. Like any fantasy, it serves your purposes alone. It has no standing in the real world which we share with each other. Those character traits, those attitudes, that behavior—that strange and alien stuff sticking out over you—that's the real you!*

Your *image*—in the context of public communication—is something you must come to know. Working with clients, I use videotape extensively to determine the effectiveness of an existing *image.* More precisely, I use videotape to work with the client in making such determinations since the effort is a cooperative one.

I do this by creating situations that match the communication challenge to be encountered as closely as possible. If it is a hostile television news interview, I learn as much as I can about the reasons for that press interest, immerse myself in details of the

---

*"What You See Is the Real You," *New York Times,* October 7, 1977.

client's business, and then with our cameras rolling, play the role of a ruthless inquisitor.

If the chore ahead is a major speech, I tape the client delivering a draft of the planned address. If the goal is better interpersonal communication by a manager who deals with recalcitrant subordinates or a physician who handles patient visits (as described in Chapter 2), then I develop an environment simulating those circumstances.

The client and I view the playback together, picking out noticeable flaws. I suggest and encourage different remedies. Although early emphasis is on the *image* of the *person,* an equal amount of attention is paid to *subject matter.* Whatever the problems displayed on the screen, the client and I work together to correct them. Success is determined by whether or not the modifications adopted do the job when viewed and reviewed on videotape.

The chapters in this book follow the same format I use when dealing with clients face to face. First, you must analyze your current *image.* If you have access to camera and recorder, begin using them immediately. If not, stand in front of a mirror to take your personal inventory. These are the areas I want you to think about, applying as a standard the impressions strangers would have of you based upon a quick meeting. In each category, consider the range as a measure of achievement and excellence, with the number 5 equaling the most and the number 1 applying to the least.

Good Looks	5( )	4( )	3( )	2( )	1( )
Voice Quality	5( )	4( )	3( )	2( )	1( )
Style of Dress	5( )	4( )	3( )	2( )	1( )
Physical Presence	5( )	4( )	3( )	2( )	1( )
Intelligence	5( )	4( )	3( )	2( )	1( )
Extrovert-Introvert	5( )	4( )	3( )	2( )	1( )
Wit	5( )	4( )	3( )	2( )	1( )

Confidence	5( )	4( )	3( )	2( )	1( )
Social Status	5( )	4( )	3( )	2( )	1( )
Ethnicity	5( )	4( )	3( )	2( )	1( )

You will have a second chance to assess yourself in each of these aspects of your public *image* as we explore, in depth, how they affect your success as a communicator and the ways changes can be made to reduce or eliminate negative qualities.

I call these changes the creation of *illusions!*

4 Illusions

The news director had just hired an anchorman at a television station where I was working. "You should see him," the news director said. "What a hunk the guy is. Great looks, voice like a bass drum, outstanding presence on camera, acts like he owns the world . . . "

"You're forgetting only one thing," a writer interrupted sardonically. "The guy doesn't have a brain in his entire head."

"Don't concern yourself," the news director shot back. "You'll write the words we put in his mouth, and the audience will think he's a genius."

That's the world of television for you. It is also a realistic approach to professional public communication. No one merits a 5 in all of the categories listed in our "Image Profile." If you judged yourself as being less than a superstar when it comes to extroverted personality, readiness of wit, or physical presence . . . what then?

The answer is *illusions,* and the talent to create them. That capacity represents the significant difference between amateur and professional communicators. Professionals know how to create *illusions* of the *image* that will best reinforce the message they are delivering.

The Illusions of Professional Communication

Illusion is a loaded word. Applied to a magic act, it has a positive connotation. We accept and even are delighted to be fooled in an entertaining cause. But when the word *illusion* relates to the scams perpetrated by an unscrupulous used car dealer, then it becomes sordid and shameful. I'd like you to think of the term in a positive light, and I believe you will as you read on.

The easiest way to introduce *illusion,* as it applies to communication, is to share with you insights about how the most polished of communicators—entertainers—use illusion in their performances.

There's No Biz Like Show Biz

You fly to Las Vegas to see the shows (and maybe even gamble a bit). Headlining at your hotel are a superstar singer and a comedian known for off-the-wall zaniness. Plunking down thirty bucks for admission and a watered drink, you settle into a seat hoping to be entertained. Fortunately, you are. The show is a winner (which is more than you can say about your run at the slots). Maniacally original, the funnyman convulses the house. When he loses balance during a dance sequence, bumps into the chorus line, and knocks his toupee askew in the bargain, the audience roars its amusement.

And the superstar singer? He certainly gives his all. So much so that at one point he has to loosen his tie, unbutton his collar, and sit on the stage apron to rest up before the next medley.

A superlative two hours, well worth the price of admission. But you witnessed strictly the front-of-the-curtain version. The real show lay in the performers' ability to convince each spectator that his performance was spontaneous, one that developed in the excitement of that particular show. If you were to stay on for the second show, you would observe 120 minutes of comedy and song virtually identical to that presented during the first.

Esquire magazine ran a fascinating article about entertainer Wayne Newton, which highlighted this difference between illusion and reality.* Newton has become a Las Vegas phenomenon. Other stars may be well received and attract huge and admiring audiences, but Newton's enormous earnings made it possible for him to buy a casino outright.

Ron Rosenbaum, the author of the *Esquire* article, contends that Newton's success lies in convincing every audience that it is special and entitled to an extraordinary effort from him. He apparently accomplishes this with a nightly routine in which he thanks the spectators for their enthusiastic response, saying he is so energized that he is going to work harder, longer, and more feverishly than normal. "[Newton] begins playing on the expectation of something special happening, the dream that tonight some magic suspension of the rules is in the offing—the ultimate unpurchasable Vegas experience." In effect, although the attendees may have lost at craps or roulette, they are winners at the Newton show, getting bonus chips in return for the paid admission. The marvel, according to Rosenbaum, is that "each of the twelve shows I saw started and ended at the same time *on the dot.*" The whole performance, including the promised extra effort, is a *show.*

I first began to understand the *illusion* perpetrated by entertainers while still in my teens. As a devoted fan of Judy Garland, I trekked to New York to catch her performance at Carnegie Hall. She lived up to all my expectations. She was absolutely brilliant. Part of her appeal centered on her long-term emotional relationship with the American people. Part was talent. The mix of ingredients produced pure magic.

Midway through the concert, Garland forgot the words to a song. Struggling to recover, she mumbled and fumbled and made up lyrics. The struggle lasted a full minute before she finally got back on track. We cheered and applauded her recovery. The

---

*"Wayne Newton, Do You Know Vegas?" by Ron Rosenbaum, *Esquire,* August 1982.

moment dramatized the touching vulnerability Garland always managed to convey.

Later that same year, I saw Garland when she brought her show to Atlantic City's Convention Hall. The Convention Hall production equaled the one I had seen at Carnegie Hall. It should have. It duplicated the former, note by note. Even to the moment when (you guessed it), Garland forgot the same lyrics to the same song in the same place at the same time. I couldn't believe my eyes and ears. Even "failure" was built into the act. Garland knew that, in her later years, audiences came as much to see if she would rally from well-publicized bouts with booze and drugs as to hear her sing "Over the Rainbow." A professional to the core, Garland understood what she was selling.

You have every justification to say, "Hey, that's show business and has little to do with a speech before the Rotary Club." Well, we'll examine that very shortly. First, direct your attention to the most believable folks you watch on your television screen—newspeople. Everyone knows the names listed on the nightly news credits belong to working journalists, interested in providing the facts, just the facts. TV news organizations certainly make that point often enough. Now let's look at the facts.

News Biz as Show Biz

Consider this: You are an admirer of Dan Rather's ability to deliver the "CBS Evening News." It is obvious he has a fine grasp of the material. Notice how easily he looks down at the script only as a refresher, and then reels off two or three paragraphs of the story before having to consult his notes again.

Fact: Dan Rather has both a script and a teleprompter at his disposal. Whether looking down at the desktop or directly into the camera, the copy is right before his eyes. A reflector system permits print to roll in front of the lens so that Rather can focus at the viewing audience and not above or to the side of the camera as was done when TV technology was more primitive.

An amusing anecdote from television's early days concerns Don Hewitt, now producer of "60 Minutes," then supervisor of the evening newscast. Teleprompters had not yet been developed.

Hewitt, unhappy with the way anchorman Douglas Edwards had to keep looking down to read information, reportedly suggested to Edwards that he learn braille. The idea, of course, was that Edwards would run his fingers over the raised symbols and thus keep looking into the lens. Edwards declined to accept the educational opportunity.

It is also common knowledge that CBS News executives spent the first year after Rather replaced Cronkite fiddling around with the background setting, lighting, and the anchorman's clothing in an attempt to soften his somewhat intense appearance. Indeed, the highest ratings for Rather's program seemed to come when he wore a V-neck sweater on the air. What the sweater had to do with his ability as a journalist is an intriguing question. So is the one about whether Rather is paid in seven figures a year because of writing and editing talents or his ability to attract viewers.

Consider this situation: Your local mayor is interviewed by a TV reporter about a possible tax increase. Onscreen, the reporter is seen skillfully asking questions, never flubbing or faltering.

Fact: The interview is conducted with only one camera, which remains on the mayor's face throughout the session. Afterward, the camera is turned toward the correspondent, who re-asks the questions while looking into the lens. If the first take is sloppy, the reporter may take as many attempts as necessary to make it perfect. Back at the studio, the film or tape editor creates the illusion of a fluent reporter, the image you see at home.

There are additional media illusions in Part Four of this book. At this point it is enough to say that news is not the only business of a TV newsroom. Former correspondent and presidential press secretary Ron Nessen described his own impressions of these bastions of journalism: "Everywhere I went, I saw anchorpersons—men and women—devoting the crucial 30 minutes immediately before air time not to gathering and writing the news, but to applying makeup on their faces and spraying their hair into immobility."* The point is that TV newspeople and nightclub comics have much in common. They both practice the art of *illusion.*

---

*TV Guide, December 2, 1978.

Lecture Biz as Show Biz

I turn finally to the type of communication situation that may most closely parallel your own: addressing an audience of ten or one thousand. Have you ever attended a convention or a meeting where a professional lecturer such as Art Buchwald or William Buckley served as keynote speaker? Have you then had occasion within a one-year period to witness the same person in a different environment? Does anything stand out in your mind? Chances are you heard essentially the same routine the second time as the first. Like politicians, paid communicators usually have a storehouse of material that they recycle repeatedly. Depending upon the audience, they may select different file cards, but totally new scripts enter the repertoire slowly. What lecturers present are rehearsed routines that appear to be impromptu. The spontaneity is an *illusion*. Great performances—in comedy, music, or speeches—are rarely ad-lib. They just appear so. Instead, every gesture is rehearsed down to the stuttered phrase or raised eyebrow.

I belabor the issue of *illusion* intentionally. More than any other quality, the willingness to practice *illusion* in public appearances marks the difference between accomplished presenters and neophytes.

Novices approach an audience with preconceived notions centering around personal ego, identity, and reality. "I know who I am," says the novice. "I'm vice-president of this, a director of that. I will just be myself, and everything will work out splendidly."

Veterans reply, "Nonsense! Worry about being yourself onstage and you are sure to fail. When I step before an audience, I don't have time for that kind of baloney. If I concerned myself with the real me, I could never smile at the same line two shows a night, six nights a week. I could never sing the same song six hundred times and make each rendition appear fresh. Imagine my having to really be original each time I crack wise. Why, I could never tell a joke more than once. My mind would wander to irrelevancies . . . like the material I'm delivering or to whom I'm delivering it. Listen, novice—professional appearances are all *illusion*, carefully rehearsed and contrived to work with the precision of a digital watch. Go before the public with that real-self approach, and you are going to get slaughtered."

That happens to be the truth. When I work before groups, I am always quick to reveal that the man they are looking at is not "the real me." It can't be. What they are seeing is a professional, Arnold Zenker, doing his professional routine. That is what I get paid for. Whether I had a scary flight, a bad night's sleep, or a fight with my assistant is not the audience's concern. Nor should it be. Their only concern is the quality of the presentation. But since, as a human being, I may very well have had a scary flight, a bad night's sleep, or a fight with my assistant, the only way I can guarantee quality is through standardization. The *illusion,* of course, never hints at standardization, but it is the reality of a professional appearance.

On several occasions, clients have mentioned experiences in which they had to speak in front of a large group on short notice with a tall hangover. Naturally, they contend they were terrible. They don't quite understand that a professional attitude toward public speaking would have spared them this public humiliation. Because a pro has planned everything in advance, personal weariness or minor irritants can be overcome.

Preaching the importance of *illusion* subjects me to an enormous amount of client resistance. I am not surprised. Businesspeople, schooled in details, react to this doctrine as anathema. The executive vice-president of a major trade association vehemently protested to me the use of such "chicanery." I quote a few lines from his letter because the point of view is typical and his concerns sincere.

"You seem to be saying a person should change his or her basic personality and character during an appearance, and I find this difficult to accept. I think a person must be honest and open in any appearance, whether on television or in conversation with another person, and I have the feeling that, over time, the playing of a role that is not your own will serve against you rather than for you."

I appreciate the anxiety reflected in those words. In part, I agree. I, too, think that honesty and openness is essential to good communication. The difference between us is that he thinks the two traits require spontaneity.

If the *real you* is so uncomfortable during a public appearance that the audience begins to feel uneasy, is that the type of honesty you wish to practice? If the *real you* creates an impression of wordiness and lack of direction during a speech, is that openness beneficial? If the *real you,* to be blunt, bores the hell out of people because of a collection of negative traits that training could alleviate, is there an argument you can make in favor of staying the way you are?

My own philosophy is that the essence of communication honesty is turning your weaknesses into strengths so you put on the very best show possible.

A client once said to me, "I have information of value to offer. If they don't want to listen, that is their problem." But if listeners turn off, are your words being heard at all? It is analogous to the philosophical concept about the tree falling in a forest. If no one hears it fall, did it make any noise when it toppled? If signals go out but no one tunes in, does it make any difference that signals were ever sent? When you address an audience that because of your own ineptitude has drifted into a coma, you might as well have saved your breath.

Remember my telling you that I have been called, sometimes with scorn, an "image doctor," "image maker," and "image priest" (whatever that means)? Inherent in the label is the implication that somehow I have the ability to mold clients into someone they are not. I am presumed to have the capacity to, with a stroke of my magic wand, create totally new identities. Unfortunately, my powers are considerably more limited.

What my job really consists of, and this book aims at, is helping you become not phony or superficial but the *best you*—a you that is as animated, dynamic, and impressive as the range of your talents permit.

The process begins by taking a more detailed look at the *image* of you that others currently have, as reflected in your answers to the questions in the Image Profile on pp. 26-27. We will examine the implications of each characteristic and how it affects your ability to communicate professionally. As I do with all clients, I will suggest concrete remedies—*illusions*—to alleviate problems, or at least camouflage them. Then we can cover the broad categories of public communication—television and live stage appearances— and explain the techniques you can use to master each.

PART TWO

Packaging the External Image

5 Vanity, Vanity, Suffering Humanity

Good Looks   5 ( )   4( )   3( )   2( )   1( )

Evaluation

Look carefully at yourself in the mirror. What do you see? Is the reflected image that of a person who is tall or short? Fat or thin? Handsome or plain? Apply the proper yardstick in arriving at a conclusion.

Be candid, but not overly critical. We all have a tendency to compare our looks with those of Robert Redford or Bo Derek. Trying to measure up to such competition is absurd. Unless you are auditioning to be a model or film star, no observer judges you in those world-class terms. Instead, we are ranked by much more pedestrian criteria, such as how we compare with an observer's own family and friends.

In our workshops, participants often downgrade their own physical appeal with comments like, "With a nose like mine . . ." or, "Old baggy eyes, here." Ninety-five percent of the time, the group claims never to have noticed the "offending feature" until it was brought to their attention. So take a hard look at yourself, but not a hypercritical or self-destructive one.

Interpretation and Action

It is unfortunate that physical attractiveness counts so much in the way we are perceived by others. In a utopia, beauty would be recognized for what it is—a gift of nature with no intrinsic value, certainly no value you earned or created. Our society understands this distinction rationally, but blurs it in practice. Sociological studies confirm this. Repeatedly, participants attribute affirmative characteristics such as intelligence, warmth, and grace to good-looking people. Even more startling, test subjects indicate a marked preference for friendship with the handsome and the beautiful.

Now, as I cautioned, your goal is not to compete with models or film stars. If most of us had to meet that challenge, we would spend our lives hiding in mirrorless, dark rooms.

The point is that negative physical characteristics can create negative impressions. We may appear older, wearier, or homelier than necessary. When unsightly traits can be eliminated easily or corrected, they should be. To live with an unnecessary indignity is masochistic.

Still, that's what people do. I think back particularly to two people with whom I once worked.

Ugly Ducklings?

I remember her well. She was about twenty-seven years old, with dark curly hair framing very pretty features, beautiful eyes, a good complexion, and a mole the size of a shaved dime on her upper lip. Whenever I looked at her, the unsightly blemish jumped out.

As the workshop day ended, I cornered her in front of the room and offered an honest compliment on the practice speech she had done earlier. In my judgment, she had solid potential as a communicator. Then, offhandedly, I asked why she had never gotten rid of the mole.

"Funny," she answered, "I've thought about it and the surgery is no big deal. It all just seems so vain."

I remember him well. About fifty, he was pleasant-looking in a plain, weathered sort of way. But his dark, heavy tortoise-shell eyeglass frames dominated his face, making it difficult for anyone to appreciate his inner warmth and vitality. At one point during the training session, I had him remove his glasses to get a look at his face on videotape. What the camera revealed gave me a clue about the glasses. Later, in a private moment, I asked how badly he needed his corrective lenses. Shamefacedly, he replied, "I don't need them at all. I wear the frames to hide these awful bags under my eyes."

"Have you thought about corrective plastic surgery?" I inquired.

He looked at me peculiarly and said, "I've heard about the procedure, but I don't think a man should be so vain."

Again and again, I hear my clients denounce "vanity." Men, especially, delude themselves into believing that showering, deodorizing, shaving, and hair combing suffice when it comes to creating an attractive appearance. But there are also an astonishing number of women who are not much more aggressive in pursuing comeliness. In cities like Manhattan, Los Angeles, and Miami, where beauty ranks with godliness, "prettying up" is treated as a science. Puritan America, in the Midwest and Northeast, remains ambivalent at best about the subject.

There was a time when I shared the attitude that we should play only those physical cards dealt to us. From childhood on, we are all deluged with the message that it is inner qualities we should stress, not external beauty. Fortunately, I went to work in television, a career experience that quickly shattered that idealistic misconception.

My selection as substitute for Walter Cronkite happened in such an extraordinary way that I never had time to give any thought to image. With scarcely an hour's preparation, I sat in the anchor chair, the red light blinked, and I began reading. I wore glasses because my nearsightedness made the print on the teleprompter too blurry to read. I wore panstick and eyeliner because a makeup artist slathered me with it, just as he did to Cronkite before every newscast. I wore the clothes I had in my closet: good, solid, styleless, executive garb. If memory serves correctly, advice from the top did come down after the first broadcast urging me to buy some blue shirts and send the bill to CBS. But that was the extent of it. No one in the department expected me to be on the air long enough to worry about. And I wasn't.

When I jumped from work behind the scenes and joined WBZ-TV in Boston as a news anchorman, I continued in the same fashion, or more precisely, lack of fashion. Astonishingly, the management at Group W offered not the slightest critique of my appearance or how I might better it. It took months before time was made available for me to view my performance on videotape. Only then did the shock hit home. I looked terrible. I looked ugly. I looked boring. The person on the screen did not have the charm and vitality I wanted to project.

Within months I changed everything. Gone were the glasses, replaced by contact lenses. Gone was the old wardrobe in favor of sportier, more show biz–type clothing. And gone was the short hair that made me look like an ROTC cadet. Instead, I had my hair styled and wore it longer. The change was dramatic enough that the program manager told me his wife spotted this new anchorman and wondered who he was. By the time I went to Westinghouse's WJZ-TV in Baltimore to host a talk show, I had achieved some of the patina of a TV personality.

In the same way, you have to decide how your appearance, as you have evaluated it, adds or detracts from what you wish to communicate. Working with clients, I am always conscious of how subtle changes, easily made, can enhance dramatically an impression of youth and attractiveness.

Easy Alterations

Hair—Women

> *The hair is the finest ornament women have. Of old, virgins used to wear it loose, except when they were in mourning. I like women to let their hair fall down their back; 'tis a most agreeable sight.*
> —MARTIN LUTHER,
> TABLE TALK

Many men declare the first thing they notice about a woman is her hair, and the way she wears it. Yet, businesswomen do their best to diminish its impact. *The Managerial Woman,* * and the articles it spawned have had a tremendous effect. Their basic message: Downplay sex. Don't be suggestive! Don't call attention to yourself! Conform! Since long hair is sensual, cut, disguise, or otherwise control it. Don't be too artsy or elaborate in styling, lest you appear too fastidious about your looks.

I take issue with this. Sensuality for a female executive does not have to be negative. Neatly styled long hair can be an asset. Similarly, coloring hair is fine if done tastefully. Pick a color appropriate to your complexion and age. A platinum-blond hue is more appropriate for a stripper than a businesswoman.

As to advice on appropriate coiffures, you will have to find it elsewhere. The topic is out of my element. There are so many styles and so many variables. Find a good hairdresser and go on from there.

Hair—Men

Although hairstyle is important to men, hair itself is the more pressing concern. Well shaped around the head or sculpted on the face, it is definitely an asset. Luxuriantly growing from nostrils and ears, hair is a horror. Yet too many men don't recognize the good that can be accomplished by a deftly wielded pair of scissors.

Mustaches

I have no objection to mustaches except that most men have little idea of why they wear them. In almost every workshop I take a close-up shot of the mustached men and then, on replay, ask what purpose the mustache is supposed to serve. One answer is typical. "Gee," said a participant, "I grew it to look older. Now I am older." If you fancy a mustache, reevaluate it every so often. And keep it neatly trimmed. Otherwise, your speech will seem to come from somewhere in outer space and not from you.

---

*By Margaret Hennig and Anne Jardim (New York: Anchor Press/Doubleday, 1977).

Baldness

My father is bald and has been since the age of twenty-seven. The lack of hair never bothered him, although I do recall his once wryly pointing out the inequity of a world where a wino lying soused in the gutter could possess a full, flowing mane while he, a healthy, solid citizen, had to wander through life with a naked pate. My father was also fortunate in that his baldness did not detract from his appearance.

If you fit into the same category—bald but presentable-looking —*great!* But if those thin strands affect your self-confidence, look into giving nature a helping hand. There are numerous alternatives.

Hair pieces are much in evidence, but wearing a full "rug" is generally a bad idea. Performers who can afford the best quality and styling sometimes obtain artificial covering almost indistinguishable from the real thing. Such loving care and treatment is not available to the average man. Most of the "pieces" I see are dreadful, badly cut and colored. Instead of being an advantage, an obvious wig diminishes the wearer's stature, reflecting his sense of insecurity and shame in his baldness.

Artificial hair can be helpful if the bald area is small and on the crown of the head. A small hank is laid in and then covered over with your own. The result is natural-looking, and can make you appear years younger. Be sure the insert is real hair though, not the Dynel you see aggressively advertised.

Hair Transplants

Another safe and successful approach to remedying baldness is the hair transplant. In the punch-graft or plug method, quarter-inch-deep circles of skin are taken from the areas of the head where hair is plentiful—such as the back or side. These plugs, each with seven to fifteen follicles, are inserted into the naked patch. Basically, the technique is a superficial skin graft. Within a week, the hair can be washed with a mild shampoo. Scabs formed over the wounds begin to fall off, with total healing taking about three weeks. The initial shock of the procedure makes the transplanted hair fall out. But three months later, it starts growing again and continues to do so.

There are drawbacks to transplanting. Cost is not insignificant. Dermatologists or plastic surgeons get fifteen to twenty-five dollars or more per plug. Since as many as four hundred plugs are needed to fill a large area, the total tab is substantial. (An acquaintance always refers to his scalp as his BMW since he could have bought such a car for the price of his surgery.) Also, the bigger the gap, the sparser the covering. Still, as a permanent method of providing hair on your head, transplants are hard to beat.

Teeth

When we speak, our teeth show. If our teeth are white and even, hardly anyone pays attention to them. But if those teeth are chipped, discolored, crooked, or have big spaces between them, watch out. They can attract unfavorable attention.

In San Francisco, as of this writing, there is a dental practice that specializes in improving the appearance of teeth. Called the Center for Cosmetic Dentistry, its founder, Dr. Jeffrey Morley, was quoted in *The Wall Street Journal:* "What it comes down to is this: Buck teeth imply people are dumb. Large canines imply aggressiveness. Weak chins imply passivity, while strong chins imply a macho, studlike personality. I don't know who made these up, but the fact is they're cultural standards."*

Whether you agree with the particulars or not, Dr. Morley's underlying premise seems true. Teeth make a statement about you. Try, if you will, to name one public figure with unsightly teeth. I can't think of any. Why? Good teeth are linked to success. Their appearance can make or even break a career. I have spoken with executives who refused to hire qualified applicants because their teeth were a turn-off. Fortunately, those who are not born with "pearly whites" can acquire them.

Orthodontia

Orthodontia is useful in sustaining the life and health of teeth, and in improving their appearance. It is now common to see grown men and women walking around with a mouth full of wire appliances. If you have buck teeth or a bad overbite or a weak chin

---

*June 16, 1982.

line, orthodontia can help. The care is expensive, ranging well into the thousands of dollars. It is also worth the price.

Caps

Another expensive proposition, "capping," involves slipping a perfectly shaped and colored jacket over the prepared natural tooth. The advantage of caps is that they can make tiny teeth larger, larger teeth smaller, and all teeth brighter and cleaner. Only teeth that are visible ever have to be capped for cosmetic purposes. You are never too old for this procedure.

Bonding

A newer technique is "bonding." In essence, appropriately colored material is bonded to the natural tooth, filling in gaps or covering permanent stains.

According to Dr. Morley, putting your mouth into harmony with your body has important psychological benefits. I believe it. Often, I see clients who have developed the habit of hiding bad teeth by refusing to articulate or smile or by keeping a finger across their mouths while talking.

With cosmetic dentistry these defensive postures are unnecessary. If your teeth display you poorly, consult your dentist about what is involved in making them a more successful advertisement.

Eyeglasses

Remember that eyeglass frames cover nearly one-third of your face. Style can make a noticeable difference in whether you seem open or secretive, young or old, pleasant or stern. When making a selection, be aware that:

- Similar shapes emphasize one another. If your face is noticeably square, offset it with oval or round frames. A round or oval face benefits from squared or angled frames.
- The upper part of the frame should follow the shape of your eyebrows and rest just above the brow line.
- A long nose looks shorter in a frame with a low bridge piece. A broad nose appears slimmer with a dark-toned bridge.

- Close-set eyes look wider in frames with a neutral colored bridge and dark side bars.
- If the lenses are thick, avoid wireless frames. Instead seek plastic frames to hide the milk-bottle effect.

Many frame choices are now available. Yet it is rare to find a person who owns more than one pair. It is akin to limiting yourself to one pair of shoes for all your business, casual, and sports activities. Consider purchasing different frame types so you can change them depending upon where or before whom you are appearing. For example, spectacles that do the job adequately in the office may not work before a television camera.

Fit

Make certain your glasses fit well. Holding a mirror at arm's length, check whether the lenses are large enough so your eyes can be seen easily. Audiences draw conclusions about us from eye contact. Eyes blocked by frames don't communicate.

For the same reason, avoid tinted or photosensitive lenses indoors; bright lights darken the glass making the wearer appear sinister. Shades are appropriate for mob leaders, not public speakers.

Have your frames adjusted regularly so they tightly grip the face. Otherwise, wear double-sided tape on the earpieces. Watching spectacles slowly slide down a nose is distracting to viewers.

Color

The color of frames is important to your appearance. A neutral shade that blends well with your skin and hair tone is attractive. Metallic rims lend an air of friendliness and ease. Dark colors, especially black, imply rigidity and severity.

If you are uncertain about what looks best, take along a close business associate to help you choose. Even better, seek out opticians who use videotape recorders. That way you can see yourself as others see you.

Whatever your choice, tailor it to your own needs. A style made popular by a celebrity may do a disservice to your own features.

Contact Lenses

I have worn contacts successfully since 1968. It is my own peculiarity that I cannot work an audience wearing eyeglasses. While perfectly comfortable with them in other situations, psychologically, specs get in the way of my reaching out to a group. Contacts allow me both to see and be seen.

I am fortunate in the ease with which I wear contact lenses. With no discomfort, I can switch from glasses to lenses and back again, regardless of whether an hour or a week has elapsed. Others are apparently not as lucky. Many try contacts and then give up the game because of pain or sensitivity.

If you believe you look better without eyeglasses, the technological advances made in contact lenses offer good news. The soft variety has proven safe, efficient, and very comfortable. Some models can be kept in the eye for weeks at a time, even while sleeping. Though hard lenses were a disaster for you, one of the newer models may not be. Consult a qualified ophthalmologist or optometrist.

Skin

A bad case of acne is devastating to deal with in adolescence. If the malady leaves behind a deeply pitted face, the condition can be equally disturbing in adulthood. Not only women suffer the embarrassment of a marked complexion. I have known scores of middle-aged men who resent and quietly suffer from this indignity. Rough and reddened skin is not a pretty picture.

For males, a beard is a way of concealing the skin problems beneath the hair. For either sex, there is now also an option called "dermabrasion." It is a simple procedure that can be performed in a dermatologist's office. A rapidly rotating brush literally sands off the pitted layer of skin. Local anesthesia makes the treatment painless, though there can be some discomfort during the period of healing. Within two months, a new smoother skin appears.

Dermabrasion can produce positive results although a reputable physician will warn that it is not a cure-all, only an improvement.

There have been other advances in treating skin disorders. One is the use of the drug tetracycline for adults with complexion problems. It controls roseacaia—reddening, swelling, and scarring of the nose and area around it. Called "rum nose," the disease is popularly attributed to overuse of alcohol. But coffee, tea, or other hot beverages, by dilating blood vessels, also aggravate the condition. Tetracycline, taken orally, alleviates the problem virtually within days. Again, consult your doctor.

Saggy Eyelids

None of us escapes the ravages of aging. As the years pass, the smooth tightness of outer skin gives way to flabbiness and wrinkles. Excess flesh in the eyelids can push them down, producing a sleepy look.

Blepharoplasty, or eye tuck, involves excising unattractive flabby skin from the eyelids. The operation takes one to two hours and is done under local anesthesia. Following surgery, the eyes appear more open and wide awake. One can return to a normal routine a few days after treatment.

Face Lifts

This is an elaborate operation and I mention it only to complete the circle of cosmetic options. In the total treatment, the surgeon smooths out deep wrinkles, tightens jowls, and banishes double chins. Incisions are made at the hairline and in front of the ears so scars are barely noticeable.

Improving on mother nature is an indulgence people are increasingly exercising. In 1982, four hundred thousand Americans, many of them men, underwent cosmetic surgery. The number is double that of a decade ago.

If you are considering a surgical procedure, take time to find a qualified doctor. Check for certification by the American Society of Plastic and Reconstructive Surgery. It tells you that extensive training standards have been met. Find a specialist. The expert in transplants may not do many nose jobs. Ask for recommendations from your friends, colleagues, or your personal physician.

Recognize the risks. Infection, permanent numbness from cut nerves, bad scars, and even problems with anesthesia are all possible complications. Mistakes in plastic surgery are not uncommon and can produce the unkindest cut of all.

The Body

The American craze for physical fitness shows every indication of becoming a permanent part of our national character, a development for which we should all give thanks. A fit body is a healthy body; medical studies show definitively that an exercised, weight-controlled torso is less subject to ailments such as heart disease, high blood pressure, and diabetes. A fit body is also an asset in presenting a winning image.

Picture the healthy person: perfectly tanned, thin and fit, even though middle aged. The impact on others? A lithe figure communicates that its owner works at good health and is vital and confident.

Picture the unhealthy person: pasty, paunchy, and drooping, with a body that looks ten years older than it actually is. The impact on others? A flabby, fat figure communicates that its owner has a low self-image and lacks drive and determination.

There are numerous books and exercise and nutrition clinics to help you with the process of getting into shape. If you suffer from obesity or flab, consult them.

What you can improve immediately is posture. Besides causing digestive and orthopedic problems, poor posture makes you look your worst. Slouchers look shorter, less sharp, and less confident. There is one easy remedy: Stand up straight. Don't puff out your chest like a pouter pigeon, just stand up straight and you will instantly appear younger and more assertive.

Willingness to Change

The format of a training program I conduct for a major corporation brings together all students in a group for a day of introductory instruction. Thereafter, the group is segmented into private, more tutorial, sessions.

In one of these workshops, I noted two participants with interesting mannerisms. One blinked his left eye repeatedly in a nervous twitch. The other never spoke without first loudly clearing his throat. By chance, both these individuals shared the same private session.

Delicately, I inquired of the twitcher whether he wore contact lenses. Sometimes they can be an irritant. When he said no, I videotaped him and pointed out the flickering eyelid.

"My god!" he exclaimed. "I never realized I did that."

"Why, Joe," said his colleague, "I've known you for three years and you've always been an eyelid batter."

"Why didn't you tell him?" I asked, even though I knew why. We don't tell people about their annoying mannerisms out of politeness. We also don't criticize because we fear it will make us subject to evaluation ourselves. Which brings me to the throat clearer.

He at least knew about his trait and had a good explanation. "I have sinus problems," he said. "I tend to fill up. I've been to the doctor about it, but he says nothing can be done."

Fair enough. We live within the reasonable limitations of our medical problems. But then it occurred to me that he only "filled up" at the beginning and end of sentences. When I pointed out this peculiarity, he seemed surprised. With practice, he became capable of speaking for minutes at a time, resisting the urge to clear out that mythical frog.

We often become comfortable with our own mannerisms. They are friends of long duration. Subconsciously, we loathe giving them up. That would be fine if we existed in isolation. Sharing space with others, we can't afford that luxury. Too often we just succeed in making the people around us uncomfortable.

If you have a physical characteristic that common sense dictates is an annoyance, make an effort to correct it. Don't wait until someone else is daring enough to tell you the bad news. Your improvement in communicating with others will astonish and delight you, and give you greater poise and confidence.

6 Saying It Sweetly

Voice Quality 5() 4() 3() 2() 1()

Evaluation

When we first examined *image*, I asked you to evaluate the way you appeared to others in a variety of categories. A similar test is appropriate when it comes to voice. Read the following paragraph into a tape recorder, duplicating as closely as possible your normal manner of speaking aloud.

> I am happy to welcome you to this, our company's fiftieth birthday party. In my own judgment, it has been a distinguished half century. Eldon Admas, who founded Winderscore, had a dream. His dream was to produce an alarm clock that would do more than keep time and ring on time. His concept was to manufacture a product so stylish and durable and true that it could serve generation after generation within a family. Fortunately, Eldon Admas was also a realist. When sales began to dip in the 1940s, he immediately recognized that the cause was all those old "built-to-last" timepieces,

manufactured a generation earlier. They still worked. "Fellows," he is reported to have said to his staff, "permanence is no way to build a company's sales." With that revelation, Winderscore switched to the philosophy that has resulted in the billion-dollar concern we are today: "Make it so that someone can break it."

Now play back the tape and listen closely. Here are some criteria to consider.

Is the vocal sound loud or soft? Pure or raspy? Well articulated or fuzzy? Nicely paced or too fast or slow? High or low pitched? Expressive or flat?

More generally, what is the overall impression a stranger would have about a person with such a voice? Age? Level of education? Regional background?

Interpretation and Action

Many years ago, while still single, I attended a network party at an elegant restaurant in Manhattan. It was a mob scene. The crowd consisted of a few "beautiful people" and many more who wished they were. In the midst of the madness, I caught sight of a stunning young woman who looked like an actress or model. Our eyes locked, a mystical wave of current closed the gap between us, and we slowly worked our way toward each other. Eagerness and expectancy charged the atmosphere. Finally, we were close enough to begin the preliminary small talk. "Hi," I said.

"Hooy," she answered. "Wha'cha doin' heah at this foine affaah?"

To me, hopes for a new romance quickly wilted and died. Within minutes, I made my excuses and renewed the search for another pair of beautiful eyes, hopefully paired this time with a more attractive voice.

Save for our physical appearance, our voice and speech pattern define us more quickly than any other feature. A voice's cadence, pitch, and timber identify our class, education, and upbringing. It is so much a part of our uniqueness that voice prints are as reliable a means of identification as fingerprints.

Friends and family instantly recognize our voices on audio tape. Still, when most amateurs hear themselves on tape, they inevitably say, "It just doesn't sound like me." In a sense, the protest is accurate. The voice we hear echoing through our heads is very different in tone from that heard by the outside world. It is shaped by the reverberations of throat, mouth, nose, and ears, an amplification no one can experience but ourselves. We believe that the sound we hear in our heads is the way others hear us until we hear our voice on tape.

Most people don't like the sound of the unfamiliar voice on tape. It is not nearly as strong, mellifluous, or charming as they expected. So, like ostriches, they simply refuse to deal with the reality.

Some voices are so fuzzy or grating that they are inherently unpleasant. But these are few in number. Most voices detract from communication because they are underutilized. This failure is correctable.

Let me summarize briefly how vocal sound is created. It is a product of respiration (inhalation-exhalation of air), phonation (vibration of the vocal folds), and resonance (modification of tone by throat, mouth, and nose).

Respiration

Whether playing the oboe or speaking aloud, creating sound requires exhaled breath. Breathing to live and breathing to speak are quite different functions. For example, we inhale more rapidly when speaking, usually through our mouths, and we breathe at a different rhythm when we speak than when we relax. There are different types of breathing as well. Shallow breathers use the upper chest, while deep breathers use the abdominal muscles to control air output. Deep breathing is considered more effective for speaking since it provides the greater supply of air. Controlling the flow of air is the first step toward producing a full, resonant tone.

Phonation

As we exhale, the air travels through the larynx or "voice box." Inside are the vocal folds, more commonly known as the vocal cords. Vibration of these folds (as well as their length, thickness, and the muscles that regulate them) produces the changes in human voice pitch.

Resonance

If vocal-fold tone were listened to without adjustment, it would sound unpleasant, more like a yelp than the sound of the human voice. The adjustment of that tone by throat, mouth, and nose gives it a rounded quality. We call the end result resonance.

Changing the way we sound is, in part, a function of modifying breath control, phonation, and resonance—each within the limits of our physical structure and personalities. Other factors include rate of speech, articulation, and expressiveness. The last, which is the ability to provide range and quality to the voice, is most important to effective communication.

American speech patterns generally are divided into three regional variations.

Mid-American

This pattern of inflection and timing is spoken by the largest segment of our population. In the Midwest, Southwest, and West, "American" is spoken in purest form. Mid-American is distinguished, to our ears, by a lack of any accent. For years, it was the standard of speech sound required of professional broadcasters. I remember that at ABC-TV in the sixties, the staff announcer's audition included a series of readings designed to single out and exclude those candidates with any trace of regional dialect. Such speech was considered NBQ—not broadcast quality. Staff announcers, as a breed, hardly exist anymore. Neither does the emphasis on mid-American.

Eastern

Primarily found in the New England states, the eastern accent features a broad *a* and a dropping of the final *r*. At its most extreme, you "pahk that kah in Hahvahd Yahd."

Southern

States as far south and west as Arkansas and Louisiana produce citizens who prolong or drawl words and who drop the second half of a diphthong. They utter "fan" when they mean "fine" and "as" for "ice." At its best, a southern accent can be an asset, symbolizing courtesy and graciousness. At its worst, the syrupy tone can sound unpleasant and affected to nonsouthern ears.

In addition to these main branches, there are dozens of subaccents. They reflect ethnic background or upbringing in particular sections of certain big cities. The most obvious is the "deze, dem, and doze" attributed to Flatbush, a neighborhood in Brooklyn. But a trained ear can easily distinguish a native of Baltimore, Philadelphia, or St. Louis.

The crucial question is when and to what extent an accent should be eliminated. My own answer is hardly ever. If voice color and flavor are positive goals, then regional accents can help to achieve them.

ABC's "Monday Night Football" series is a calculated utilization of accent and tone to accomplish vocal contrast and dynamic tension. On the left, Don Meredith, playing Peck's Bad Boy with a Texas twang; on the right, Howard Cosell, born in the South but playing a biting, Bronx bandit; in the center, literally and figuratively, Frank Gifford, the all-American good guy. The trio's sound is unbeatable—lively, colorful, recognizable, and just plain fun to hear.

If your accent is so strong that sounds are unintelligible or so harsh that others' ears just don't want to listen to you, begin immediately to soften its most negative components. Otherwise, the accent is probably working in your behalf.

And that about sums up the standard that should be applied to overall quality of voice and diction: not whether you sound like Sir John Gielgud acting a Shakespearean role or Lauren Bacall urging Bogie to whistle, but whether your vocal efforts get the job done. Will an audience respond positively to the *sound* of your voice?

If you detect specific problems in your voice evaluation, there are solutions. A good book on using your voice effectively can get you under way; a visit to a good vocal coach is another alternative. For starters only, you might try the following exercises.

Respiration, Phonation, and Resonance

If your voice does not seem steady, muscular, or of good quality, lack of adequate breath control and throat tension are probable causes. Exercises are usually done to relax your vocal equipment.

1. Inhale deeply and then begin counting from the number one. See how far you can go before having to breathe again.

2. Again, inhale deeply, then make the sound *s-s-s.* Keep time, trying to extend the length with each effort.

3. Pant in short bursts. While panting, say, "Hah, hah, hah; he, he, he; ho, ho, ho."

Try to avoid letting out a large part of your air supply on the opening words or phrases. Instead, use only as much as is necessary to support the sound.

At all times, try to keep the throat relaxed. Strain in the neck can make the voice quiver.

4. Simulate a yawn. You should strive for a feeling of freedom in the throat.

5. Apply calming procedures such as lying on a bed, flat on your back. Try to make your limbs feel weightless. Open your mouth wide and allow the jaw to swing from side to side. Slowly say, "Yah, yah, yah, yah, yah," and variations on the same theme.

Volume and Pitch

Don't confuse these two categories. Pitch is the basic tone of your voice and is determined in large part by the thickness, length, etc., of your vocal folds. Long, thick, relaxed folds create a low-pitched tone. Short, thin, tensed folds product a high-pitched tone. I, personally, don't believe that attempting to change your pitch makes much sense. Lauren Bacall reportedly acquired her throaty, deep-toned sound through continuous yelling and screaming exercises. I don't know if the story is true, but, if so, it is a great example of extraordinary effort to achieve desired effects. If you wish to make a similar attempt, determine your optimum pitch by striking different notes on the piano. Hum that pitch regularly, and practice readings using that tone.

Volume can be improved by reading aloud, constantly testing yourself to reach different areas of a circumscribed space. For example, first try to toss your voice halfway across a room; then try to reach the wall at the other end; finally try to project so that listeners in the next room can hear you through the wall. Don't strain. A relaxed, open throat is the key. Ask a friend for assistance in judging your progress.

Here is an exercise to practice volume improvement:

> In almost every one, if not in every one, of the greatest political controversies of the last fifty years, whether they affected the franchise, whether they affected commerce, whether they affected religion, whether they affected the bad and abominable institution of slavery, or what subject they touched, these leisured classes, these educated classes, these titled classes have been in the wrong.
> —WILLIAM E. GLADSTONE (1809–1898),
> BRITISH PRIME MINISTER

Or this one:

> Communism is a hateful thing and a menace to peace and organized government; but the communism of combined wealth and capital, the outgrowth of overweening cupidity and selfishness, which insidiously undermines the justice and integrity of free institutions, is not less dangerous than the communism of oppressed poverty and toil, which, exasperated by injustice and discontent, attacks with wild disorder the citadel of rule.
> —GROVER CLEVELAND (1837–1908),
> TWENTY-SECOND AND TWENTY-FOURTH PRESIDENT OF THE
> UNITED STATES

Before moving on to speech speed, articulation, and expressiveness, a cautionary word about voice quality. There is a medical difference between voice harshness and voice hoarseness. Harshness is a functional problem; instruction and exercises can cure it. Hoarseness almost always signals an organic disease. Swelling, contact ulcers, and growths, both malignant and benign, are possible causes. Consult an ear, nose, and throat specialist if you suffer from hoarseness. Do not delay. Not recognizing and healing the difference between vocal harshness and hoarseness can be fatal.

Speech Speed

Speaking too quickly or too slowly are equal turnoffs. Listeners become just as exhausted from a machine-gun pace as from a slow delivery. Unable to follow the material or sustain concentration because of an ineffective speech rate, audiences close their ears and stay bored until the speech is over.

Determining acceptable speech speed is difficult, since there are many variables. The articulation of the speaker, the complexity of the material, and the size of the audience all play a part. There is also some confusion between duration of speech (length of individual speech sounds) and rate (number of words or syllables spoken per minute).

You will have the best chance of holding your audience's attention if you speak 135–185 words per minute. You can determine your own average speed of speech by reading the following paragraph aloud, as you would to an audience. Do the exercise several times to arrive at a true rate, using a stopwatch to record your time. (Numbers in parentheses indicate the amount of words up to that parenthesis.)

There is a significant distinction between the orator and the writer. The orator must be prepared to move a mass of men at once. The writer addresses himself to one man at a time. If Conrad had been asked to write a story for a million readers, I fancy he would have desired to reach them all and to entertain them all. But certainly he would have refused to "write down," to coarsen and vulgarize his truth, or to take the individual color and flavor out of it. His problem would have been to induce that elephantine public to incline *(100)* its great ear near enough to overhear him telling his story with all its fine shadings of truth, into the ear of one intelligent crony. That is the way good stories are told. To seize a megaphone and to become the mouthpiece of a political party, or of a church, *(150)* or of a traditional interest, or of a social class, or of the Army or the Navy, or big or little business, or feminism, or prohibition or other organized reform that is an easy and safe form of authorship, which at once insures you a constituency and a backing and a *(200)* bodyguard. It places you in the organized world. It makes you a part of the elaborate system of institutions in which we live and have our being.

—STUART PRATT SHERMAN,
AMERICAN CRITIC (1881–1926)

The above paragraph is 227 words in length. Test how far you read in one minute.

Unless you find yourself speaking either extremely slowly or extremely rapidly, I am less concerned with your average speech speed than I am with your ability to vary it. Some material, such as disclosure of bad news or a complicated fact pattern, should be delivered slowly and deliberately. Other information requires a medium pace, whereas still different types demand a galloping cadence. Professional communicators have the capacity to shift gears on demand.

Once you have determined your average pacing from the above exercise, reread it at different rates until you develop an inner sense of timing that allows you to escalate or retard speed at will.

Articulation

As a people, we Americans are notorious for using poor diction. We slur, mumble, clip the ends of words, and in many other ways sound as if we suffer from lockjaw. This is a shame, because good articulation enhances communication. It makes us more understandable. Poor articulators inevitably lose an audience. When listeners have trouble following a speaker's content, missing important parts of it because words are unintelligble, they eventually find other distractions—like timing how long they can hold their breath or counting the number of tiles in the ceiling overhead.

Good articulation makes the speaker appear more animated and more interesting. If the mouth and lips hardly move, the bottom half of the face seems frozen. Since facial expression aids in reinforcing content, poor articulation means 50 percent of the speaker's ammunition remains locked in the arsenal.

To test and practice articulation, attempt these readings. Speak them rapidly.

I wish I hadn't broke that dish,
I wish I was a movie star

I wish a lot of things, I wish
That life was like the movies are.
> —SIR ALAN HERBERT

It is easy for men to talk one thing and think another.
> —PUBLILIUS SYRUS

So, friend, we're not the folks to shrink
From the duty of giving you something for drink
Besides, our losses have made us thrifty
A thousand guilders. Come, take fifty.
> —ROBERT BROWNING

Break, break, break
On thy cold grey shore, O Sea!
> —ALFRED, LORD TENNYSON

As an egg, when broken, never
Can be mended, but must ever
Be the same crushed egg forever.
> —THOMAS H. CHIVERS

Great rats, small rats, lean rats, brawny rats
Brown rats, black rats, gray rats, tawny rats.
> —ROBERT BROWNING

He is all fault who hath no fault at all.
> —ALFRED, LORD TENNYSON

Better no rule than cruel rule.
> —AESOP

'Tis an old maxim in the schools
That flattery's the food of fools.
> —JONATHAN SWIFT

Much outcry, little outcome.
> —AESOP

On a tree by a river a little tom-tit
Sang "Willow, tit willow, tit willow."
> —W. S. GILBERT

For the moon never beams without bringing me dreams
Of the beautiful Annabel Lee.
> —EDGAR ALLAN POE

If your tongue stumbles badly over these monsters, you may have a speech impediment. But more likely, you don't articulate with sufficient clarity. Now try the same reading again, this time exaggerating mouth, lip, and tongue movements. Have another person watch you do the exercise. When finished, ask the observer whether your mouth appeared distorted. You will be shocked to learn the answer is no. You probably thought you looked like a clown, contorting your facial features so extravagantly. But that is simply because you are not accustomed to making your mouth move so much.

Now try these classic tongue twisters:

1. Esau Wood sawed wood; Esau Wood would saw wood.

2. Theophilus Thistledown sifted a sieve of sifted thistles.

3. The sea ceaseth and that sufficeth us.

4. Six thick thistle sticks; six thick thistly sticks.

5. A basket of biscuits, a basket of mixed biscuits, a basket of biscuit mixers.

6. Mother loves buttered buns.

7. Betsy Butter bought a bit of better butter and it made her batter better.

8. Moses supposes his toeses are roses, but Moses supposes amiss.

9. The sixth sheik's sixth sheep's sick.

10. Sixty-two sick chicks sat on six, slim, slick, slender saplings.

Are you having an easier time of it? Keep practicing. Improvement is easy to attain.

Warming Up

A musician preparing to perform always spends time warming up on the instrument. Playing a piano with stiff fingers or a trumpet with lazy lips is painful to do and painful to listen to. To get underway at full speed and minimize stumbling and fumbling, speakers should warm up their lips and tongue. A good exercise is:

Hub-bub-dib-dab-dabble-babble-bumble
Hub-bub-dib-dab-dabble-babble-bumble
Mumble-tumble-bumble-jumble
Mumble-bumble-tumble-jumble
Double-bubble-mumble
Double-bubble-mumble

Another warm-up game is to repeat the following words as rapidly as possible without tripping over them.

Red leather yellow leather red leather yellow leather

Expressiveness

The metaphor of the vocal apparatus as a musical instrument plays equally well when voice range and expressiveness are the objects. Johnny-one-notes, on a sax or at the lectern, are boring to listen to. The full flavor of sound is in its complexity—highs and lows, fasts and slows. The talent to run your voice up and down the musical scale at durations of a quarter-note, half-note, or full-note gives spoken language life and vitality.

Unless you are a born actor, achieving this complexity of delivery requires practice. The following selections were designed both to test your vocal versatility and to improve it through repetition and experimentation. Use an audio tape recorder in the process.

Drama/Motivation

When would the ability to express drama be useful? Suppose a regulatory commission is proposing rules that would limit your company's ability to do business severely. Or, you are trying to motivate your sales force with respect to a new promotion. Using flair and force is appropriate.

Ladies, we are here to sell cosmetics. Not just any cosmetics, but Cathy Cute Cosmetics. Why do we sell Cathy Cute Cosmetics? Because we want to make the world dazzlingly beautiful. And how are we going to sell cosmetics to the world? We are going to organize, in order to create a more perfect union of *good* products, *good* women, and *good* looks.

You owe it to the world to spread the word about Cathy Cute. Women who look better, feel better. Their men feel better. Their kids feel better. I feel better when I look at an attractive, well-groomed woman. We all feel better, and that's what we're here for, isn't it?

Many of you have been with Cathy Cute for years. Not only do you enjoy outrageously generous commissions, but, if you make enough of those sales, you are eligible for something Cathy Cute gets a lot of pretty publicity about—promotional prizes! This year the top producer in this region will receive a red mink coat, full-length, of top quality, and brandishing our little trademark, the blue collar. Another sixteen of you lucky women will be receiving a red Cadillac for your labors. Our sales director will be announcing winners later.

So, look alive! Remember it all started, for each and every one of you, with one sale. I want you to go out there and "make up" America. Let's put on a happy face!

How is a sense of flair and force created? It is not so much a matter of which words you emphasize, though hitting hard on obviously unimportant words can jar the listener's ear, but the ability to skip your tones up and down the scale and prolong key phrases. As a model, think of Dr. Martin Luther King Jr's style. "I can *seeee* the top of the mountain." Or, "Let my *people* gooo . . ." Strive to affect an extroverted personality as you practice the reading.

Light Touch/Humor

When delivering humorous material or injecting a lighthearted note, the tone must be appropriate, but in your own style, otherwise it sounds forced.

These days young people want to be free to express themselves, not just at home, or at school, but everywhere. They don't just express by writing letters to the editor, either. They have to be "creative" about it.

Just last week we were discussing instituting a dress code at *Vague* magazine. Well, one of our young ladies in Research was up in arms. You see, Miranda believes in self-expression. Sometimes she comes into work sporting bright red knee pads, army boots, and a khaki shirt. Maybe she's trying to express that her brother played hockey before he joined the Marines. Who knows? Maybe she's in the Reserves, part of an elite core of crackerjack rollerskaters.

I'm not quite sure what it is that she's trying to express when she comes in dressed like that, but whatever it is, it's clear she has strong feelings on the subject.

Most people find it murderously difficult to tell a joke or anecdote in a fashion that produces the hoped-for smile or belly laugh.
One-half of the reason for failure is the material itself. (How to
wisely select wit is covered in Chapter 14). The other half is the
actual spinning of the yarn. There is no one way to deliver humor
effectively. Rodney Dangerfield can be hilarious with a deadpan
approach; Red Skelton stretches his face and voice like putty.
When I help clients practice a piece of light material, I urge them
to concentrate on "twinkling from within." Vocal tone should be
airy—helped by a facial expression that implies you know the
punch line and the audience still doesn't. Don't rush recitation of
humor. Take it at a relaxed pace.

Bold Directness

There's no pussyfooting around when the time comes to lay
down the law. If you are lecturing employees, or going after something you dearly want, the only way to be convincing is to be
relentless with your message.

> I want to be class president. The job's main attraction, as I see it,
> is power. As class president, I would be called upon to determine
> when and where to give parties, who the judges are for prom queen,
> to which charities we donate our services, and which procedures
> determine who gets scholarship money. These opportunities spell
> power to me.
> The second plum of being CP is status. I estimate, for example,
> that I'll get 50 percent more girls to date me as CP. You might say
> my election will offset my shyness.
> Then there's the matter of getting into a good college. As many
> of you probably know, I scored a total of 550 points on my SATs.
> Being CP could be a real shot in the arm for me, admissions-wise.
> I don't think it really matters to any of you who your class presi-
> dent is. So why not vote for someone who needs your help? Vote
> for me, Forbes Xavier Carrington, class president of Topsider High
> School—Class of '84.

Straightforward material should be delivered exactly that way
—in a no-nonsense, not-to-be-toyed-with fashion. You might practice sounding angry while reading this appeal for votes. Think of
yelling at your spouse or your kid. An amateur's inherent reserve

onstage usually calms an "angry outburst" so that it comes off sounding only firm and forceful to the audience.

Warmth/Sincerity

Let the world know you mean it from the bottom of your heart when you say thank you.

> I can't believe this is *my* retirement dinner. It seems like only yesterday I walked through those big green doors for the first time.
>
> I don't want to sound too sentimental, but the thirty years I have worked at Overseas General Airlines have been the happiest, most meaningful years of my life. When I started working here I had no idea of the tremendous opportunities that awaited me. There aren't many companies that send their trainees through school or offer them so much growth. But OGA did.
>
> Why did OGA take a chance on me? I was just another kid from the poor side of the big city. Why? Because OGA is run by the right kind of people . . . real people . . . caring people . . . people people . . . people who want to make the world a little better . . . people who are willing to share their piece of the pie.
>
> Of course, I don't have to tell you this . . . because you are those people. You took the time out of your busy schedules to make this company a haven where, no matter what else was going on in this crazy, mixed-up world, I always knew I'd get an even break, at the very least.
>
> There's no such thing as a little guy at OGA—only big opportunities for anyone who wants to make the most of them. As a result of that attitude, you have enriched my life. Thank you, all of you, for giving me a chance. I'd like to think I didn't let you down.

It is easy to sound warm and sincere if you keep just one thought in mind. Imagine that your daughter is dressed in a beautiful gown for her very first school dance. She comes down the steps and says shyly, "How do I look?" The pride in your heart will translate to a tone of voice exactly the same as the one you should use when speaking from the heart to colleagues at your company or volunteer workers at the charity of which you are president. Allow a little syrup to flow. Your listeners will welcome it.

Shakespeare summed up the need for expressiveness best.

> Speak the speech, I pray you, as I pronounced it to you, trippingly on the tongue; but if you mouth it, as many of your players do, I had as lief the towncrier spoke my lines. Nor do not saw the air too much

with your hand, but use all gently; for in the every torrent, tempest, and, as I may say, the whirlwind of passion, you must acquire and beget a temperence that may give it smoothness."

—FROM *HAMLET,* III, II

You may find it interesting and effective to read and study the following books to learn about using your voice more effectively. *Voice Power* by Evelyn Burge Bowling (Harrisburg, PA: Stackpole Books, 1980); *Your Voice and You* by Jessica Dragonette (Emmaus, PA: Rodale Press, 1966); and *Speech for the Classroom Teacher* by Dorothy Mulgrave (Englewood Cliffs, NJ: Prentice-Hall, 1936, 1946, 1955).

7 Dress Code

Style of Dress   5 ( )   4 ( )   3 ( )   2 ( )   1 ( )

Evaluation

Analyze the way you dress. Would strangers characterize your clothing and accessories as high style? Shabby? Unconcerned? Pick your own adjectives. Try to be objective.

Interpretation and Action

The clothing and accessories we wear provide myriad clues about our occupation, educational level, degree of affluence, social class, political philosophy, and even ethnic background. For example, we are all familiar with the stereotypes of mob leaders, who only wear shiny silk suits and brightly colored shirts; business leaders, who dress only in blue, black, or gray pin-striped suits; and bureaucrats, who are given only to polyesters and plaids. Fair or not, dressing within these rigid styles stereotypes us.

John T. Molloy's *Dress for Success* pioneered a rush of similar books and articles, which explained in depth the career implications of wearing certain colors, styles, and fabrics. Surely these books have had an impact . . . but sometimes I question just how much.

When I look out at participants in my workshops, I see many of them wearing outfits overdue for donation to the neighborhood thrift shop. I see combinations of hues and patterns that don't coordinate. I see men wearing clothing that is oversized, undersized, and not even remotely sized for their shapes. And I see women in dresses that look like they were designed by fashion school drop-outs.

My clients are the type who read experts like Molloy. Why then do they seem to completely ignore their advice? A combination of psychological and practical causes are to blame.

"I know what I like"

It is commendable to have a sharply defined sense of taste and personal style in clothing. The phrase "I know what I like" often reflects the attitude of an individualist who doesn't wish to be dictated to by the arbiters of fashion. Unfortunately, a sharply defined taste isn't always the same as "good taste." I see executives every day who may know what they like (or what their spouses like them to wear) but who don't realize that their own personal preference in cut, color, or quality does not serve them best in the eyes of others. For example age can bring white hair and wan-looking skin. A "business gray" suit exaggerates this drabness, making the wearer seem even more colorless; conversely, the right shade of tan or blue worn with a lively tie and a smartly patterned shirt restores a sense of vitality. *I* know what *I* like, too, but I always seek a trained outsider's advice as to what style looks most flattering on me.

Conformity

America's great financial, manufacturing, and legal institutions
demand from their employees conservatism and blandness in both
personality and appearance. When Arthur Watson ordered his
managers at IBM to dress in dark blue suits with white shirts and
button-down collars, that code was only a fraction stiffer than
those in effect almost everywhere else in the business community.
While such rigid demands for uniformity eased during the 1970s,
many businesses and professions still demand a strict dress code.

I saw a fascinating example of this at the upper-management
levels of a bank for which I consult. Among the key officials was
a man I used to refer to fondly as Charlie Superstar. He was
debonair, knew it, and dressed the part. Designer labels, seen and
unseen, were in all his clothes. He really did look well turned out.
But—and this is important—everything about him was in good
taste. Had he been a television network executive, his style would
have been judged right and proper. By the style standards of his
financial colleagues, though, he dressed in high fashion.

The man's management skills were unquestioned. Even his se-
verest critics within the company praised his talents as an adminis-
trator. Yet during a period of corporate upheaval, he was eased
out. A survivor of the purge summed up the reason: "I'll tell you
what brought down Charlie. The guys in our group all dress from
Brooks Brothers. Charlie insisted on wearing Pierre Cardin." So
much for individuality in corporate life.

Cost

Fine clothing is expensive. At today's prices it is easy to spend
seven hundred fifty to a thousand dollars assembling a complete
outfit. I feel the pinch myself. Selling image two hundred days a
year requires a large wardrobe that reinforces my message. Maintaining it involves a big financial outlay. I understand fully how
individuals for whom stylish clothes and job success are not so
interrelated stick with last year's fashions.

Confusion

Another factor contributing to poor clothing choice is confusion about what is right, what is wrong, what is in, and what is out. The advice manuals, while raising sensitivities, also did their cause a great disservice by being complex and nitpicky.

Alleged authorities assert that pinstripes are okay, but chalkstripes are not; some say dark is dominant, others say dark is dull; vests are okay for men, but not for women; wraparound dresses are too sexy because they hug women's bodies. Is it any wonder that even the most highly motivated reader turns away perplexed?

I have good news for you. Dressing for a public appearance is a much simpler undertaking than dressing for your business or love life. The reason? Public appearances are sharply defined situations in which very specific goals are achieved within a finite time frame. So put aside your own personal preferences, and follow this most basic rule as you plan what you will wear at your next speech or presentation:

YOUR CLOTHING SHOULD ENHANCE, NOT CONFLICT, WITH THE MESSAGE YOU WANT TO SEND.

In our workshops I show a ten-second snippet of videotape capturing three corporate presidents in an appearance on a television news-panel program. I freeze-frame a picture of the three and ask the audience, "Do these men appear to be environmentalists . . . or perhaps consumer advocates?" The question is so absurd that the response is always laughter. Why? Because the executives are all dressed in dark blue suits with white shirts, undistinguished ties, and wingtip shoes. In making his comments, each businessman expresses concern for his customers, compassion over high prices, and respect for antipollution laws. But their clothes cried out "conservative" so blatantly that their oral messages were buried in a storm of conflicting signals.

I do not suggest these executives wear shirts that are open to the navel and gold chains around their necks. But slightly more informal clothing, or even lighter colors, might have broken their boardroom stereotypes and created an impression of contemporary concern.

So, if a particular engagement demands that you be perceived as a no-nonsense solid citizen, dress conservatively. If the desired effect is casual, sports clothing may be appropriate. Like a chameleon, change your outer skin to blend in with the atmosphere you are trying to create.

Other commonsense rules:

Clothing Must Be in Style

There is a difference between being in style and being stylish. The latter implies dressing at the vanguard of contemporary fashion. If you wish to be stylish, that's fine. But it is not essential in order to be a successful communicator. Dressing in style is.

Out-of-date clothing suggests an out-of-date person. Wearing wide lapels when thin are in, or culottes when tailored slacks are in vogue is equivalent to saying, "Look at me! I am too unsuccessful or old fogeyish or unaware to buy new clothing."

I know there are many famous people—from statesmen to stars —who feature a particular style of dress regardless of the dictates of fashion. The difference between them and us is that they can afford to. Eccentricity is permitted the rich and famous. If a Rockefeller chooses to drive a 1960 Buick, the world still knows he owns a piece of Rockefeller Center. When you wear clothing that look as old as that Buick, don't expect an audience to give you the same benefit of the doubt.

Wear Quality Clothing

Since as few as two outfits may suffice to meet your role as public communicator, blow the budget when it comes to quality of fabric and tailoring. A speaker who wears a doubleknit polyester suit right off the rack of a nationally advertised discount house is just begging to be treated as a lightweight. This may not be a nice commentary on our system of values, but it accurately reflects the impressions others will draw.

I mentioned previously that I tend to wear expensive clothing when I work. That is not a boast. In my personal life I am equally happy in corduroys, a sweater, and a shirt. But when I am before a client who has paid a handsome sum for my expertise, I better look the part of a good investment. That can't be accomplished with shoddy goods.

Do Not Imitate the Audience's Dress Style

This is a common mistake. For example, as an alumnus, you are called upon to speak before kids at your alma mater. The site is the large auditorium, the time is the middle of the afternoon. You know the students will be wearing sweaters, jeans, typical school attire. Should you attempt to match it? Of course not. Wear an outfit that will reinforce your message. If that message is "executive comes to visit," dress like an executive. You can wear a sports jacket, but don't wear one with jeans. You are not an undergrad. Pretending to look like one of the crew will destroy your credibility.

Many of my presentations are made at large conventions held in resort areas. To the attendees, the meeting is a blend of business and relaxation. I am never surprised to walk in and find an audience dressed in tennis whites or even bathing attire. I still choose to wear a suit. I am not on holiday. I am there to work. My outfit is a work outfit.

The Outfit: Parts and Pieces—Men

The Suit

Suits come in an enormous variety of styles, patterns, and colors. Although it is essential that your fashions be up to date, you don't have to keep pace with every trend. Unless there has been a clearly determined change in suit cut, such as the switch from wide to narrow lapels in the early eighties, it is acceptable to be one season behind the designers in making your selections.

Be sure your suits fit.   I have seen executives who make million-dollar decisions cowed by tailors. Assert your rights. Do *not* stand up straight while being measured. Stand the way you normally do.

Don't suck in your gut while the waist is being pinned, unless your abdomen is normally that taut. Trouser legs should touch your shoe tops in front and descend about three-quarters of an inch longer at the heel.

Be sure your suit flatters.   The average American male stands about five foot ten and weighs between 140 and 175 pounds. Variations from that norm are probably the rule, not the exception. Don't buy suits that are too tight or too baggy—either extreme makes you look like you're wearing someone else's clothes.

If you are short and wish to create the illusion of a few extra inches, wear clothing with vertical lines. Pinstripes, narrow ties, and narrow lapels all help. Also, make sure the skirt of your jacket is as short as possible. The more trouser showing, the longer the legs seem. Similarly, keep slacks cuffless and cut slim of line. Cuffs and flares cause a stubby look.

To avoid looking like a scarecrow, tall men who are very thin should accentuate the horizontal with plaids and wider lapels. Layering can also create the illusion of a deeper, broader frame. A jacket over a V-neck sweater over a tie over your shirt will provide a depth you may find desirable.

Fat men should stay away from light-colored clothing. Darker colors are more slimming. As with short individuals, play up the vertical lines. Keep your jacket closed when possible. And, make sure your tie is long enough to reach near the belt line. There is nothing more unattractive than a protruding belly with a tie ending somewhere in the middle of it.

The Shirt

Remember the days when a shirt was a little like Henry Ford's Model T? With the car you could choose any color so long as it was black, with the shirt any color so long as it was white. Then in the late sixties came the male fashion revolution and the shirt, that once conservative piece of cloth, was suddenly aflame with wild colors, stripes, and patterns in blinding combinations. Freed from restraint, the shirt now made a statement. The problem is that, to this very day, most men have no idea what it is saying.

A shirt does more than keep a necktie in place. It communicates a subtle message about who and what you are. It serves as a frame for the face, drawing attention to your good features and underplaying your weaker ones. Ideally, that is. Realistically, it often accomplishes the exact opposite. Here are some suggestions on shirt styles and how they can be utilized to improve your appearance.

The shirt must match the suit and tie. Though this rule seems rudimentary, there are many men who seem to have trouble coordinating the two. If you doubt me, just look around your own office.

One way to avoid mismatches is to purchase the shirts and ties together, preferably against the background of the suit coat they will accompany. Ask a salesperson for help. Usually, they have a flair for fashion and can help you choose an attractive combination.

Let's begin with the collar. It has three basic elements: slope, point, and spread. The slope indicates how high or low a collar rises on the neck. By adjusting the slope, a long neck can appear shorter or a short neck longer. Experiment with different slope heights until you find one that looks right. Then stick with that model.

Point refers to the length of the collar tips, whereas spread measures the distance between those tips. Points and spread can be manipulated for effect. Long points and a narrow spread will thin out a chubby face, and the reverse can broaden a skinny one. Again, experimentation and some good advice are the keys to making the right choice.

Short sleeves are as tacky as short socks. Even in the summer, wear long sleeves. The shirt sleeve should reach the base of the thumb when the arm is hanging loosely by your side. Since the sleeve will wrinkle at the elbow during use, it should fall just below the thumb joint when brand new. As to the amount of cuff that should show beyond the jacket, the standard of good tailoring allows for a range of one to two inches. It's primarily a matter of taste.

Consider the alternative of custom-made shirts. Retail stores sell ready-made shirts in the twenty- twenty-five-dollar range. For not much more than that a good custom shop can offer the options of slope, point, and fabric just right for you.

The Outfit: Parts and Pieces—Women

It is difficult, if not impossible, to offer generalities about clothing styles for women. Certainly, some of the suggestions on the preceding pages apply equally to both sexes. Clothing should be stylish, properly fit, and in keeping with the individual figure.

But whereas businessmen are still basically limited to suits, shirts, and ties, businesswomen have a virtually infinite supply of clothing combinations to feature. Suits, skirts, sweaters, blouses, slacks—put them all together, add the colors of the rainbow and different patterns, lengths, and shapes, depending on the fashion of the year, and the complexity of the recipe becomes quickly apparent.

Although most women generally have a good idea of what clothing becomes them, it is not a talent possessed by all. In dressing for the public spotlight, wear whatever you think will best announce your sense of self-confidence and worth. That confidence will translate into a convincing and effective presentation of the the information you are presenting.

If you're comfortable wearing a dark suit with a contrasting blouse and maybe a scarf, fine. If another style serves you better, fine too. Dressing fussily or in apparel that is too eye-catching is out—you don't want to give the impression that you missed your calling as a model for *Vogue.* But make sure that everything you wear or carry is of the best possible quality, and preferably of natural materials, like wool, cotton, and silk. A vinyl handbag is no substitute for a good leather one. Your shoes and purse add touches almost as important as your clothing.

Don't attempt to live up to the standards of models or movie stars. What looks like a knockout on Lauren Hutton may look like a knockdown on you. *Who do you want to be? How do you want to be perceived* before an audience of strangers? Dress to make that perception come alive.

One Final Thought

One final thought about clothing: Take care not to allow your mood of the moment to dominate your clothing selection.

Often, upon awakening in a sour mood, we feel inclined to wear the oldest, shabbiest outfit in the closet as if, subconsciously, we wish to proclaim our discontent to the world. Similarly, if we dislike the customer or the product we are pitching, our selection of clothing can echo our misery. *Don't fall into this trap!*

Objectify clothing choice. In fact, when glum, choose the brightest, happiest clothing you own. It may well fool the world into thinking you are upbeat, and that helps to get the message across.

You may find it useful to read these books about effective dress: *Dress for Success,* by John T. Molloy (New York: Warner Books, 1978); *You Are What You Wear,* by William Thourlby (New York: New American Library/Signet, 1978); *The Managerial Woman,* by Margaret Hennig & Ann Jardin (New York: Anchor Press/Doubleday, 1977); and *Image Impact: The Aspiring Woman's Personal Packaging Program,* by Jacqueline Thompson, (New York: Ace Books/Grosset & Dunlap Co, 1981).

8 The Rest of the Package

We have explored the importance of physical attractiveness to a positive *image*—attractiveness in the sense of being well groomed, well dressed, and well spoken—and the *illusions* available to aid in creating positive impressions in each category. But these are not the only traits that trigger audience response. There are also key personality elements, touched upon in the "Image Profile," that spark audience perceptions. Before elaborating upon the techniques that can bolster these, you should rank yourself again in each category. As always, the number 5 and number 1 refer to measure of intensity, not best and worst.

Physical Presence: 5( ) 4( ) 3( ) 2( ) 1( )

Physical presence refers to the use of your stature to command attention. Presence can be related to attractiveness, but the two elements do not always go together. There are people of imposing height, good looks, and sturdy physique who, when standing in front of a group, fade right into the wall. Conversely, there are the short and roly-poly who exude an aura of size and strength. All of us have had the experience of seeing an F. Lee Bailey type, for example, take over a room at will. Bailey is about five foot six, but in court or on the stage, the famous lawyer appears to be much taller. He knows how to be imposing, impressive, dramatic. Creating a sense of physical presence is a learned technique. Mastery of it greatly enhances your communication skills.

Intelligence: 5( )   4( )   3( )   2( )   1( )

When we attend a presentation, we desperately want to hear a speaker who is learned and thoughtful. We resent having to put up with the uninformed platitudes of a dolt.

Appearing intelligent or well educated does not depend upon possessing a high I.Q. If it did, most of us would forfeit the game before it begins. Instead, being judged brilliant and literate is a function of knowing how to tie together preparation and delivery of material. Put another way, in a given place at a given time under controlled circumstances, just about anyone can appear to be bright and effective.

Extrovert-Introvert   5( ) 4( ) 3( )   2( ) 1( )

In our training sessions, I am quick to point out to clients that I have little interest in whether they are personally outgoing or shy. But, when it comes to public appearances, I have a definite preference.

Extroverts stand a far better chance of capturing and holding a listener's attention. Audiences want to feel emotionally involved with the presenter. Extroverts seem to reach out and embrace all within their presence.

Mood variety—the ability to fluctuate in delivery style—is crucial to communication. The outgoing have a greater capacity for switching from displays of sharp-edged firmness to ebullient good humor.

If your demeanor is dry as burnt toast and you have to be

hugged to be heard, you are fighting an uphill battle in engaging a listener's concentration.

Wit: 5( )   4( )   3( )   2( )   1( )

The ability to turn a clever phrase or evoke the most laughter out of an amusing anecdote is an asset. All top professional communicators work hard at incorporating humor and wit into their routines. Chapter 14 analyzes how amateurs can make the most of this specialized talent.

Confidence: 5( )   4( )   3( )   2( )   1( )

In my first on-air radio job, I pulled the weekend shift at a medium-sized station in Wilmington, Delaware. Only a skeleton staff worked the weekends, and we did everything including answering the phones. One Saturday, a caller requested the weather report. "Wait a minute," I said, shuffling through the pile of papers in front of me. "I just had the darn thing . . . hold on until I locate it." The report refused to surface, and the delay and apologies increased. Finally, I found the forecast and read it to the caller. The station manager happened to be visiting. When I hung up, he said, "You handled that poorly. This is a radio station. When a member of the public calls a station for information, they expect definitive information. It would have been better to look out the window and immediately say 'fair and sunny or cloudy and wet'; at worst you would have been proven wrong four hours later. You can't communicate authority by hemming and hawing, ducking and dodging, and if you don't project authority people turn off."

His advice, in part tongue-in-cheek, has always seemed to me transferable to a speaker's relationship with an audience. Pauses and equivocations, although a normal part of daily conversation, tend to come across as uncertainty or even evasion during a public appearance. An audience pays attention to a speaker who exudes sureness and confidence.

Social Status and Ethnicity:
5( ) 4( ) 3( ) 2( ) 1( )

In America, we have a very muted sense of social status. Our democratic heritage restrains us from appearing too elitist, or for that matter, too lowbrow. I remember a college sociology professor making the point that only in this country does such a large percentage of the population refer to itself as middle class. Physicians who earn a six-figure income and laborers who take home only a tenth of that amount are equally likely to represent themselves as members of that vast middle stratum.

At the same time, ethnicity has come back into favor. Although a generation ago, people changed their names from Wojdyslawkski to Witt, DePasquale to DePaul, Rabinovitz to Robin, today they proudly are proclaiming and retaining ethnic heritage. Author Irving Wallace's author son, David, for example, uses the original family name Wallechinsky.

A good communicator has the ability to alter signals of social status and even ethnicity, depending upon audience composition. Politicians are masters of this.

Boston, where my firm has its offices, is a highly tribalized city. Contained within a small geographical area are "Brahmins," whose ancestors founded Boston and still control its financial power; the Irish and Italians, who subdivide themselves by both neighborhood and political activity; the black community; academia; and a self-contained medical population.

Come election time, and any candidate running citywide must appeal to each of these groups. I have worked with aspiring officeholders who can instantly clothe themselves in the social traits of the market segment they are working. One candidate whose roots were in South Boston (home of the working-class Irish), but whose congressional district encompassed upper-class Brahmin territory as well, constantly fascinated me with how deftly he could change stripes according to the region in which he campaigned. When he approached home turf, his South Boston tongue turned so thick I barely could understand a word he said. But when he spoke before members of the Bar, the tones became strictly Harvard. Incidentally, he captured his district and still serves.

In a like manner, a French actress and television personality who used to guest occasionally on my interview program confided that every two years or so she would take lessons to assure her French accent retained its flavor. She rightfully viewed that accent and her trick of humorously corrupting the English language as money in the bank.

I don't seriously argue that the average person should bend an image quite as sharply as the politician or performer, but it helps to be aware that playing up or rounding off the rough edges of class background or ethnicity can increase listener receptivity.

Action

Before proceeding, I think it useful to pause here and recap where you should be at this juncture.

- You have made the effort to explore the *image* you currently create in the minds of others. You recognize this self-evaluation as crucial because you are convinced that a large component of any communications triumph depends upon the perceptions an audience takes away about *you*.

- In an objective, nondestructive manner, you have pinpointed the characteristics of your external package that hinder your ability to get a message across—in a "live" presentation or on the television screen. You already are working on improving easily changeable components, such as negative physical qualities, poor voice projection, or inappropriate style of attire.

- Still unclear in your mind is how to begin enhancing those other *image* characteristics discussed in this chapter—intelligence, confidence, wit, etc. The tools to accomplish this involve understanding and shaping a great many forces—like the willingness to "act," peculiarities of specific types of communication forums, the structuring of material, the ability to set the stage, and the talent to control an interviewer or an audience. Providing you with these tools is really what the rest of this book is devoted to. Let me introduce the next sections by discussing "acting."

Effective communication utilizes four elements—information, facial expression, voice variety, and body language. To the extent the four unite in a common cause, the message is reinforced. If they operate at cross-purposes, the message is muddled.

As an example, keep your facial muscles frozen and say, "I am happy to be with you this afternoon." Try to make the statement meaningful, using vocal expression alone. Now try the same statement again, this time with a big smile on your face. Notice the difference. It is virtually impossible to *sound* happy unless your face acts out the same emotion. Try the statement one more time, adding body language. The overall effect will be even stronger.

Good radio performers acquire the talent of combining face, voice, body language, and information early in their careers. Even though no one is watching their labors, they play out every word. On radio, TV, or in a speech you must follow the same practice. When I say this, a common response by clients is: "That's great, but tell me how to do it. Can I walk around the stage or wave my arms during a speech? May I move at all during a television appearance? Can I really use my face to 'mug' different emotions?"

The answer to all these questions is: *yes,* if the activity is highly planned, rehearsed, and disciplined. Your thought process should center on why, for example, you are striding around the room and gesturing. Is it to play different segments of the audience and animate your material or mainly to discharge nervous energy? The former is fine; the latter an unacceptable practice. Similarly, a facial expression that seems realistic and believable to a person watching you from the tenth row of an auditorium may seem overdone to a home viewer staring at a closeup shot on the television screen. It's all a matter of being a good "actor."

To most nonprofessionals, *actor* or *acting* are dirty words. However, good acting, in the context of public communication, means matching face, voice, body, and content for maximum impact. If you perform without thought and preparation, it will appear under or overacted.

The way to become a good actor is to practice, practice, practice —looking at yourself on videotape or listening to yourself on audio tape while gazing into the mirror. Exercises of the type I included in Chapter 6 will stretch your capacity. It is also helpful to act out your interpretation of a particular presentation in front of a coach. I function in that role for my clients, but a family member or friend will serve you as well.

Acting effectively helps to create the *illusion* of a controlled, intelligent, extroverted person who knows what he or she is talking about. So does knowledge of the mechanics used by professionals to produce an appearance for TV or the rostrum. Sections Three and Four cover these two worlds. I have chosen to separate them for purposes of clarity, but it should be obvious that there is much overlap in the techniques advised. Be aware of that as you read on.

PART THREE

Facing Up to It

9 Socking It to Stage Fright

If there is one universal experience shared by public communicators, stage fright has to be it. No matter which group I work with or which client I counsel, sooner or later the question always emerges: "How can I avoid feeling nervous when I have to go on television or make a speech?"

One evening, on a plane from Washington, D.C., to Boston, I sat next to a young man whom I recognized immediately, although I never acknowledged it. His mother, whom I also recognized, was seated one row ahead. Her presence confirmed that they were members of a famous American family.

We began to make small talk and the youngster indicated he and his relatives were on the first leg of a weekend ski trip to Sherbourne, Vermont. He asked what I did for a living. When I explained, he showed intense interest. It turned out that although only seventeen and a prep schooler, he often made speeches. On one memorable afternoon, he had actually talked to four different groups. But he regularly got the "cold and clammies." "Is there a way of getting over such fear?" he wanted to know.

I suggested a few approaches. He listened intently, and then quite seriously asked for my business card. Normally, such a request from a teenager would provoke an inner smile. But the young man was Chris Kennedy, son of Robert Kennedy, and I can only assume this was a classic case of planning ahead.

When the spotlight beckons, not only public communication neophytes get upset stomachs; veteran performers tremble as well. Singer Carly Simon stayed off the concert stage for five years because facing live audiences paralyzed her with fear. One of the musical theater's great stars, Gertrude Lawrence, lamented, "These attacks of nerves seem to grow worse with the passing years. It's inexplicable and horrible."

Any Hope?

Before writing this chapter, I read dozens of books about public speaking, curious to see what others recommended as cures for stage fright. To my surprise, I found most authors dealt with the subject superficially or not at all. In her 1970 book *Speech Can Change Your Life,* Dorothy Sarnoff, an acquaintance from my days as a television talk-show host and current competitor in the communication-counseling field, devotes exactly one-half page to the subject. She concludes that "speech confidence comes from knowing that you have something worth saying, and that you can say it in a way worth listening to."

Other writers offer advice equally noncontroversial, such as keeping your energy level up, getting a good night's sleep before the big event, and avoiding involvement in another complex project at the same time.

Considering that stage fright affects so many, why is there so little advice about overcoming it from authorities? Because, until now, there never has been a "magic pill" that really provided relief. The best any of us could suggest, including me, were nostrums for controlling general anxiety.

Stage fright is, after all, just nomenclature for the "fright and flight" response we experience when confronted with a threatening situation. Our hearts beat faster; adrenaline flows; blood pressure rises. External manifestations are sweaty palms, weak knees, parched throat, tense muscles, and an overall ill feeling. At its worst, the reaction can be so great that temporary paralysis and fainting can result.

I said there has been no real remedy for stage fright *until now.* Medical science has finally discovered a "magic pill" that appears to be highly effective. You will find its name in the last pages of this chapter. But don't skip this section to learn it. In the long run, it is healthier if you can control stage fright by understanding and preparing for it. Bear with me while I point out the basic psychological cause of audience panic and how commonsense tactics can defuse it.

The Cause

I am convinced the roots of audience anxiety almost always can be traced back to about the fifth grade in school. The teacher assigns each student the chore of writing a three-minute speech on "How I Spent My Summer Vacation" or some other stirring topic. A few kids, the born showoffs, tackle the project with glee. The remainder view it with dread. Making a speech in front of classmates, especially at that age, immediately subjects the youthful presenter to ridicule. Any mistake and there will be catcalls, snickers, and snippy remarks.

The moment of truth arrives. Students make bloopers. Does the teacher skillfully minimize the discomfort? Sadly, no. Too often, the adult adds to the misery with either a harsh evaluation or a pointed jest that produces hysterical laughter. Scarred to the soul, each child sits down and swears never to stand before an audience again.

Quite reasonably, none of us enjoys public failure and the embarrassment that accompanies it. Facing an audience expands our vulnerability. Our intellect, bearing, diction, and appearance—our very ego—is exposed to critical judgment. Who welcomes such a risk?

The Core Cures

Recognize That Your Audience Has a Positive Attitude Toward You

Audiences want you to be a winner. If you doubt this, think of the last presentation you attended. Did you wish the speakers failure? Of course not. Failure means the listener pays the price —enduring acute boredom. If you give an audience a good show from the start, their initial good feelings blossom into approval and acceptance.

Come Prepared

I will stress the point while discussing television; I will hammer it home again in the section about "live" stage appearances. The better prepared you are, the more successful you will be. Visualize the absurdity of winging it: I am sitting in that airplane with young Chris Kennedy, and a voice comes over the intercom. "Mr. Arnold Zenker, please report to the cockpit immediately." I march forward, nervous about the reason for the summons. "Mr. Zenker," says the pilot, "will you please substitute for the navigator? He is ill." I panic at the prospect.

A ridiculous example, you think. Maybe. But I will tell you, from experience, that amateurs tackle public appearances with little more preparation than I would have as a fill-in navigator. Just as a veteran pilot feels at home in the cockpit, so does the prepared communicator feel at ease on a television program or standing at the lectern.

Before stepping front and center, know your material cold, practice it extensively, familiarize yourself in advance with the surroundings, and stay glued to your own scenario.

When you are properly prepared, it is the audience that should be nervous. *You* know what you are going to say and how you will say it. *You* decide when to show slides or call a break. *You* are the one in control. As Ethel Merman put it when asked whether she got nervous while singing on Broadway, "Me get nervous? They paid twenty-five dollars a seat; let them get nervous."

Put a Little Calm in Your Life

While awaiting your introduction, it is effective to practice deep breathing. Take a slow, long breath, drawing the air into your lower lungs so that your stomach expands. The deliberate activity and the extra oxygen are calming.

Sit still and think of a gently flowing brook. The relaxed body posture triggers the brain into signaling all is well. Adrenaline flow is reduced; tranquility increased.

What about liquor as a relaxant before going on? Not for me. I am not making a moral judgment. I simply can't handle any kind of alcohol before working an audience. It dulls my senses and takes the edge off my timing.

I suggest you experiment. If a drink or a glass of wine calms your nerves and still allows you to speak clearly and effectively, then by all means indulge.

Stay away from milk or other dairy products before an appearance. These coat the vocal folds, creating an urge to constantly clear your throat.

Hamming It Up

Stage fright ceased to be a problem for me in high school. Elected to the school's tribunal, I had to speak three lines to the assembly. I never considered carrying a crib card. As an aspiring actor, I had memorized huge scripts. Who needed the crutch?

Me! I blanked out completely. Titters began to build. A personal disaster loomed. Then the humor of it struck me, and I began to laugh. Surprised, the audience laughed with me. Such shared good feelings helped me recall the three lines. I spoke them, sat down, and have rarely been nervous since.

Having a sense of humor about yourself and your failings may be the *best* way to conquer stage fright. Trying constantly to present perfection onstage is an impossible task. Reveal your own rough edges to others, and the relationship is easier and more rewarding on both sides.

And Now for the Name of the Magic Pill

It's called propranolol. One of a class of drugs known as beta blockers, propranolol apparently diminishes nervous stimulation of the cardiovascular system, thereby reducing the manifestations of "fright and flight." It is widely used to treat angina and high-blood-pressure patients.

An experiment conducted at New York's Julliard School of Music and the University of Nebraska revealed propranolol's value as an antidote to stage fright. Twenty-nine musicians gave two recitals for critics and teachers. Before one recital, each received a dose of propranolol, before the other a placebo. The results were dramatic. The average rate of heartbeat during the performance under the effect of propranolol—104 per minute—under the placebo, 148. Reportedly, the audience favored the calm performances induced by propranolol.

What are the risk factors? Not much. Propranolol is not a narcotic, so it can't addict you; it is not a sedative, so you don't become drowsy. But it can be dangerous for people with certain ailments, such as asthma, hay fever, and diabetes; and it produces, as do most drugs, some minor side effects.

I raised the issue of safety with doctors participating in a workshop I conducted for the American Academy of Family Physicians. They concurred that I could recommend propranolol, a prescription drug, with the clear warning that you should consult your own doctor before using it.

Suppose, in spite of your best psychological efforts and even a dose of propranolol, you still find yourself "clutching" in front of an audience. Then what? Try not to show it. If there is a lectern nearby, hide your quaking body behind it. Keep your hands pressed firmly against the wooden surface. Slow down, breath deeply, get your thoughts together. As far as the audience is concerned, you are only nervous if they know you are. Hide the outward symptoms of stage fright and the secret will be yours until calm returns. It always does.

PART FOUR

On the Tube

10 Introducing the Spectacular Machine

I believe television is going to be the test of the modern world, and that in this new opportunity to see beyond the range of our vision, we shall discover either a new and unbearable disturbance of the general peace or a saving radiance in the sky. We shall stand or fall by television—of that I am quite sure.

—E. B. WHITE, 1938*

Television is chewing gum for the eyes.

—FRED ALLEN**

Nothing is real unless it happens on television.

—DANIEL J. BOORSTEIN***

Television, now in its fourth decade as a mass medium of communication, has turned out to be exactly what its boosters and critics predicted it would be . . . and more. A saving radiance in the sky, chewing gum for the eyes, informational, outrageous, entertain-

*From *Removal,* cited in *Harper's* magazine, September 1960.
**Quoted by George F. Will, *Newsweek,* January 10, 1977.
***New York Times,* February 19, 1978.

ing, and mind numbing, television is, most of all, an inescapable part of our lives.

In the years ahead, TV will be even more intrusive. Advances in technology, such as satellites and cable (transmission of programs and information to our homes across coaxial wire instead of via the airwaves), have given birth to new entities like HBO, ESPN, and CNN, breaking the thirty-five-year monopoly of the major networks in determining our viewing choices. Already the capacity exists for two-way cable, where the viewer can figuratively talk back to the telecaster. This infant science figures to play an important role in the way we eventually learn, shop, and bank.

The business world is making a giant effort to utilize the benefits of this explosion in video capability. Most large corporations have equipped their training facilities with television studios; smaller organizations possess at least basic hardware. The options for usage are multiplying.

Video is assuming the function of imparting job information to new employees; recruits seem to absorb the material more quickly this way, perhaps because watching the home screen has conditioned them to do so. Chief executives of conglomerates with geographically dispersed divisions are reaching out to on-site managers by closed-circuit television rather than by telephone alone.

Teleconferencing, via satellite, is permitting companies to set up their own networks for one-time meetings or sales demonstrations, broadcast to customers or employees throughout the country or the world. My own firm has found a new market in helping produce these teleconferences, and in training executives how to appear in them effectively.

Considering the limitless future of the medium, I am always startled when organizations shy away from television training on the grounds that it is irrelevant to their day-to-day activities. To the contrary, it is quite possible that average businesspeople, who never dreamed of showing up *on camera* will do so at one time or another. Everyone in the marketplace must come to understand how to best take advantage of the medium as a tool of internal communication. Although the information included here should help you in that regard, it is not the thrust of this section. My main concern is helping clients cope with the experience of becoming *stars*, often involuntarily, on commercial television, especially news programs.

Business and Television News

Americans watch television six to eight hours a day and rely upon it for the main part of their news and information diet. Fifty-five million tune in every evening to major network newscasts; twice that number sit through one or more of the local station offerings. In spite of the time we put in as viewers, most of us remain in the dark as to how news programming is produced. This unfamiliarity can create a sense of acute discomfort when businesspeople have to participate in the game as subjects. A call from Mike Wallace, or one of his local counterparts, often is considered terrifying, and there is a widely held belief (with some justification) that TV journalists distort facts and conclusions for the sake of sensationalism. A complaint I hear repeatedly is, "Why can't those b——— do *positive* stories?"

Understandably, the sensible executive prefers that only "good" stories ever be broadcast about his or her organization; but such an expectation is, to put the matter gently, unrealistic. For example, I fly at least a hundred thousand miles a year. When Delta is ready when I am, United's skies are friendly, and American is doing what it does best—who cares? That's what we all expect. But when an airplane "unexpectedly loses altitude," to use a euphemism favored by flight attendants, the crash is legitimate news.

That is because bad news sells. There is simply more public interest in disaster and nasty gossip than in stories about "white hats and stout hearts." If you doubt this, compare the viewership of a well-balanced but bland documentary program on public television to that of "60 Minutes." The gap in favor of the CBS News product is so large that there is no contest. For the network, or any news program, ratings convert into revenue dollars and profits—giant profits. Only a fool believes that news producers are unaware of this relationship when making decisions about what events to cover and how to cover them. According to Dan Rather, the "CBS Evening News" seeks "the kind of thing . . . that evokes an emotional response. When I go back to the [control room], I tell them, damn it, we've got to touch people."* The way to do this, of course, is with drama. As Walter Goodman wrote in the *New York Times*, "Where would '60 Minutes' be without its bad guys? '28 Minutes'? Give a television producer your lame, your halt, your blind, and he'll give you an affecting hour . . . a talking head is an invitation to a channel switch, unless the head has eyes that tear and lips that quiver."**

Put simply then, good news for the TV press is bad news for its subjects—in the sense that bad news can be defined as vivid and attention getting.

Paradoxically, television, properly utilized, can be a great asset in helping major institutions reach their respective constituencies. Because news and information programs have a tremendous appetite for material, a skilled communicator who can speak knowledgeably and entertainingly about a timely topic attains easy access to the TV screen.

The oil industry, for example, consistently places its leadership on the air. The instant a political question of significance to the industry such as deregulation of prices arises, a cadre of prepared speakers is immediately called into service to blitz media talk shows.

Big business utilizes other counteroffensive tactics as well. Among them: a quick request for air time to voice opposing opinions to perceived unfavorable editorials; and production and distribution to stations free of charge of entire programs featuring a particular phase of commerce. (The chemical fertilizer industry got good coverage out of what seemed to be an impartial documentary narrated by well-known newsman Martin Agronsky. Agronsky later was criticized for selling out his journalistic credentials.)

A utility in Illinois, incensed by what it claimed was a damaging and slanted "60 Minutes" report on the cost of construction of its

---

*Quoted by Ron Rosenbaum, "The Man Who Married Dan Rather," *Esquire*, November 1982.
**November 14, 1982.

nuclear facility, produced a forty-minute videotaped reply, which aired on public television stations and was written about in the press.

In financial terms alone, the benefits of a successful appearance on television are staggering. If a company receives fifteen minutes of favorable treatment on a network news program, the value is the equivalent of a multimillion-dollar free advertisement. Indeed, Coors Beer traced a substantial increase in sales to a flattering segment on "60 Minutes."

Local airtime, although not as valuable on a one-time shot, can be very important cumulatively. As part of our own service, we often train spokespeople from a company or industry to be part of a media/speakers bureau and then solicit exposure for them on local news and information shows. A study for one client showed that fifteen-minute appearances on TV shows in just four markets (Sacramento, Pittsburgh, St. Louis, and Columbus) were worth the dollar equivalent of over twenty-three thousand dollars.

What dollar figures cannot measure is the impact of getting across a message in an effective, systematic, and coherent manner. It is the opportunity to say what you want to say instead of being in the position of reacting constantly to bad news.

So, learning to handle television becomes essential for individuals and organizations both in counteracting bad press and establishing a favorable impression. The first lesson involves demystifying the medium.

11 Learning to Love Show Business

To the amateur confronting camera, microphones, lights, technicians, and correspondents, the overwhelming confusion of the television environment seems as alien and threatening as a visit to another planet.

I gained insight into how exotic the scene can appear when a business client sat in the control room during a videotaping segment. The director called out to camera technicians, "Give me a one-shot; give me a two-shot." Bewildered, the executive asked me to explain those esoteric terms. It amused me to tell him that the language was "highly technical." A one-shot means the camera is focused on only one person, a two-shot on two people.

A long-time friend and customer, John J. Molloy (vice-president, communications of Com/Energy, a utility holding company in the Boston region), once wrote, amusingly, in a newsletter my firm published about what a corporate chief executive officer experiences when he participates in the television game:

> It's all downhill from the station entrance on. Passing through some
> sound sets, the cameras seem to be following him, and the lights are

too bright. For the first time outside his own bedroom, someone has the effrontery to suggest the boss might want to comb his hair, and that he needs makeup to overcome a case of New England winter-time-paleface syndrome.

The interviewer is nice enough, though. The boss has seen him many times from the other side of the camera, and is comforted by the sense of familiarity. They chat a little bit about home and family. Later he finds out this is a ploy to warm up his features, which have gone into a deep-freeze as he realizes there are a lot of eyes out there looking at him, and that he can't see them.

Suddenly, there's a deadly silence, and even more lights blink on. The boss is in a completely different world, and reaches out toward his "friend" to continue their talk about home and hearth. But his "friend's" face has changed; maybe the lights did it. The interviewer's eyes glint, and his teeth seem to grind. The boss vaguely hears himself being introduced, and jumps slightly at the sound of his name.

"Mr. Smith, perhaps I can call you John," the interviewer's voice begins disarmingly. "I've been reading some of the reports sent over to me by Ralph Nader, er, I mean, your PR department. Tell me, how do you manage to rip off your customers year after year and get away with it?"

The rest of the interview is a blur. It goes on for what seems like three hours, yet the clock on the receptionist's desk shows it took only ten minutes.

To the unseasoned, unprepared executive, ten minutes of participation in a television interview program can seem like an eternity. There is a reason for this. Just consider the threat implied by the massive equipment. There is a peculiarly invasive quality about the camera, that impersonal metallic monster. There are equal terrors in the blinding batteries of lights, thick cables snaking along the floor, ubiquitous microphones, jaded crew members —all making up a veritable sea of quicksand just waiting to suck you in.

Whittling the television experience down to size requires a thorough grounding in the landscape. Let's begin with that before we move on to the subtle control techniques that help assure survival even during the most contentious of interviews.

Demystifying the Medium

In my experience, businesspeople too often believe they are linked by umbilical cord to the program facilities and therefore are able to affect them. So they worry about whether cameras are alive and which one to look at; they worry about whether microphones are adequately amplifying; they worry about the meaning of hand cues from the floor crew. And the more they worry about these extraneous factors, the less time they have to concentrate on the main concern—what they are saying and how well they are saying it.

When in the TV environment, try to understand that some elements are totally out of your control. The technical side is one example. Simply trust to the technicians' expertise that a decent picture of you will show up on the home screen, your voice will be heard at a reasonable volume, and the segment will have a beginning and ending that make sense. Should that turn out not to be the case, console yourself by recognizing that you personally could not have changed it for the better anyhow.

The Studio

In a studio situation, there will be two or three cameras shooting the action. Ignore them. Play your comments in the direction of the conversation. It is most disconcerting to a home audience when, out of the blue, an answer is directed to them instead of the actual questioner. A good interview presents the illusion of a discussion upon which the listener is simply eavesdropping. Leave it to the director to move around cameras so that a full-faced view of you is available.

Always assume all cameras are alive, all the time, until you actually exit the studio. Otherwise, you may be embarrassed, e.g., the moment you scratch your nose will be when the camera has you in a close-up shot.

I had a wonderful opportunity to drive this point home while conducting a workshop for a group of family physicians. One of my techniques is to grill participants in a simulated "Face the Nation" format, videotaped for later replay and analysis. In my most bar-racudalike fashion, I really laced into one of the panelists, accusing the medical profession of being con artists and callous to the needs of patients. When I finished my cross-examination, I moved down the line to the next victim. Thinking he was off camera, the in-furiated doctor gave me a rigid middle-finger salute. Of course, we caught it in on tape, and the playback offered a hilarious exercise on the dangers of letting go, even for a moment, while on televi-sion.

There are opportunities for you to adjust eyeglasses or mop a perspiring brow even while the red light is on. Arrayed across the studio will be monitors (closed-circuit television receivers). Before the segment begins, get a sense of the one most conveniently within your view. When that itch needs scratching, sneak a peek. If you are not on screen and believe you won't be for an instant, make your corrective move quickly. Please be careful not to be-come transfixed by staring at your own image. More than one amateur has been caught with a silly facial expression announcing, "Look, Ma, it's me on TV."

On Location

If the interview is conducted on location—your offices or another site—only one camera will be used. That camera will remain on your face throughout the entire segment. Subsequently, the came-raperson will shoot the interviewer, who will re-ask questions or mug facial reactions to your already on-tape answers. Editing will produce the illusion of a two-camera shot.

One-camera situations present a unique set of problems. Unless an intermission is scheduled (the next chapters deal with such control tactics), there is little opportunity to relax and compose yourself. Also, the camera will be positioned to feature a three-quarter profile shot of you, as if in conversation with the reporter.

The human face, as you probably know, is asymmetrical. In some individuals, the difference between right or left profile is very slight; in others, it is dramatic. One side can often look younger, more pleasant, or more attractive. If you have access to video equipment, tape yourself from different angles for comparison. Otherwise, scan existing photos to pick up clues about which side of your profile shows better. Try to position yourself so your best side is on camera.

To the extent you can, and in contrast with the studio situation, try to deliver some portion of your response directly to the camera. Tape clips of only fifteen to thirty seconds in length will show up on the evening news. A profile shot limits eye contact with the home audience; eye contact helps sell thoughts. Cheat and play that lens. The interviewer may not approve of your behavior. Do it anyhow. Your job is not to meet the reporter's needs, but your own.

In Studio or On Location

Microphones

Ever notice how some people feel they have to lean into a microphone to be heard. Often they glance at the instrument, as well, fearing that if they aren't looking it isn't listening. Nonsense! Once a sound check has established the proper level of amplification for your voice, don't think about the mike again. Getting adequate sound is a technician's problem, not yours.

Mikes will be attached to your lapel, blouse, or tie; they will dangle overhead from a boom, lie next to your elbow affixed to a stand, or be draped by cord around your neck. The connection makes no difference. Speak in normal, conversational tones. Just remember, vocal animation is up to you. A microphone can only amplify what it receives.

Technicians

A TV technical crew is made up of forty-hour-a-week lifers. I mean no disrespect. Some of the most competent individuals I worked with in the business were engineers. But after a certain period of time, these jobs become highly repetitive and nonchallenging. They rarely serve as a launching pad to higher positions within the company or industry. Thoroughly bored, technicians are capable of sleepwalking right through a taping. The next coffee break is more important than the on-air action.

I point this out so you will not be disconcerted by the offstage activities of the crew. Expect to hear laughter from behind the cameras, even though nothing funny seems to be happening. The laughter is not aimed at you. What probably occurred is that one crew member whispered a joke to another. Expect considerable noise. Crew members will noisily shuffle in and out of the studio, taking care to kick over props or slam the door. Expect absolutely no response to your comments, no matter how brilliant or aptly put. The techs have heard it all before.

In essence, be polite to the crew when first meeting them. Then drop an opaque curtain between yourself and that beehive of irrelevant activity only ten feet away. Concentrate on your own level of participation. That is what the home audience will see.

Makeup

Anyone who is going on air should wear makeup. That is one statement I can make categorically. A youthful, beautiful Brooke Shields might get by without it in a pinch. Don't you risk it. Even good-looking young actors wear make up without taking it as a threat to their virility.

In television, the lights are hot; the camera's image harsh. Every blemish, unsightly growth of beard, or darkening under the eyes will show, especially because TV directors like camera shots that reveal the bead of sweat on the upper lip, the welling of moisture in the eyes. They spell the essence of dramatic television. A star, growing long in the tooth, can and will demand that the camera be maintained at a medium shot, neatly hiding wrinkles and sagging skin. You have no such opportunity. So you must wear makeup.

For men, the hitch is twofold. First, should you have the audacity to ask the show staff for makeup, you will be told it isn't necessary. The reason it isn't necessary is that (except in stations where a makeup artist is required by union contract) no one wants to be bothered applying it. Yet it is unlikely that you will feel comfortable doing the job yourself at home and then walking through the streets already made up. For the laymen, such a thought is too bizarre.

The solution is to go to your nearest drugstore (or send your wife, sister, or girl friend) and buy a small cake of pancake makeup. It comes in different shades for different complexions. Purchase a color compatible with yours. If you are confused, ask the sales clerk for help. The makeup applies with a wet sponge. Five minutes before walking into the studio, or welcoming a news crew to your office, head for the men's room and lightly dab the stuff on. While not as effective as a professional job, the pancake will smooth the look of the skin, hide blemishes, and reduce oil. Carry a tissue with you to pat your face down occasionally while under the lights.

I assume most women understand how to apply makeup. Just in case, though, a few tips: A basic principle is to use the coating for sculpting. Light surfaces can be made to appear bigger and closer; dark ones recede and become less prominent.

Makeup specialists stress the eyes, lips, and cheeks. Eyes stand out better when dressed with eye-liner pencil on upper and lower lids, eyeshadow extended up to the brow, and dark mascara. An eyelash curler helps eyes look larger. Use a brush to outline lips before filling them in with color. Avoid garish reds and oranges. Blush or rouge should be applied from cheekbone to hairline.

The major distinction between makeup for street and for television is that TV requires a matte, natural finish. Accordingly, use a foundation (nonoily) only if your skin is blotchy or if one area needs particular attention. Use a moisturizer or skin toner under the makeup and finish the job off with a pat of translucent powder.

Do not overdo it. The camera can bore in so tightly that a face too heavily made up will look artificial and diminish your credibility.

Eyeglasses

We covered the impact of eyeglass frames on your ability to communicate in Chapter 4. When it comes to television appearances, there is some additional information you may find helpful.

TV lights are bright. Poorly positioned, they can produce a

blinding glare on the lenses that makes the eyes virtually invisible. If you can get through a television situation without glasses, consider doing so. Don't concern yourself that friends at the office or your family at home will think you phony. You are not playing to them, but to thousands, maybe millions of strangers watching you on TV who have never seen you before. If not wearing your glasses appeals to you, be certain to remove the frames fifteen minutes before showtime to allow your eyes to adjust and the pinch marks on your nose to disappear.

If glasses are a necessity, there is a processed lens available from your optician that can help reduce reflection. It is a multicoated glass developed by the Hoya Company of Japan. Sheen is diminished from a normal 8 percent to 1 percent. Since the treated lens is almost perfectly free of surface shine, the image is cleaner, fresher and warmer. A bonus benefit is greater visual acuity thanks to increased light transmission and elimination of ghost images. Harry Truman is reputed to have worn glasses of this type during his 1948 presidential campaign.

The lenses must be glass, a product shied away from by many people because of its weight. The solution is to have two pairs of spectacles—plastic for daily use, the treated-glass variety for those moments in front of the camera.

Clothing

Everything said in Chapter 4 about mode of dress applies to TV appearances, as well. Here are some additional factors to keep in mind.

Your outfit should be neither too dark nor too light in color. Deep blues or charcoal grays disappear into the background and the face jumps dramatically forward. Unless you are an unqualified beauty, the effect is too stark.

Very light-colored clothing, the hues you might wear during the peak of summer, creates a different problem. In reducing automatically the glare from your suit, the camera lens will muddy your complexion. The best approach is to wear colors in the middle range—tans and blues are especially effective and attractive. Shirts and blouses can be cream, blue, or yellow. A modest check or pinstripe is fine. Stay away from business gray or green unless you're satisfied to appear like a cadaver. Warm tones look best on color TV.

Stay away from tight-knit weaves or stripes, such as herringbone, houndstooth tweeds, or cords. The interaction of the weave with the picture signal will create what is called the moiré pattern. Every time you move, the fabric will seem to dance. The effect is similar to watching someone through a small mesh screen.

Wide-block plaids should be avoided unless you want to look like a fullback on the Packers. Television generally adds about ten pounds to your weight; plaids increase this problem.

Women should take care to avoid distracting jewelry. Bangle bracelets, long earrings, or anything else that gleams, swings, clacks, or demands to be fiddled with are strictly taboo. Since the camera will focus mostly on your upper torso and face, dramatic jewelry can seem overdone. The audience should be interested in the person not the decorations.

Watch professionals on the screen and you will note how often they violate every one of these rules. The difference is that professionals are at home in the medium and the audience is at home with them. After twenty years of watching Johnny Carson, his fans have a fixed perception of the man. You, on the other hand, have limited access and exposure to the medium. Your one shot on the evening news may be your only one ever. Play every angle and make the most of it.

12 Before the Red Light Goes On

Our telephone rings and the voice on the other end of the line projects panic. Some event has thrust the speaker into the public spotlight, and a "60 Minutes" crew is seeking an interview. Can we help?

We can! I say that with assurance because it's my business, and I know that the media interview situation can be controlled.

Can we guarantee a triumph over the "evil" forces of the press? Not always. If a television reporter or program wants to trash you, there is little the victim can do about it. Control of the cameras and editing equipment determines what ultimately appears on the air.

Sometimes the choice boils down to this: Should the client consent to the interview, hoping that a good performance will mitigate the almost guaranteed negative slant of the rest of the piece —or simply refuse to appear on camera? Generally, the former is preferable. But there are circumstances when silence is the wisest course of action.

I doubt very much you will ever find yourself in such a messy situation. More likely, exposure will come when a talk program invites you to be a guest on the show because of your special expertise, or a reporter requests a brief explanatory comment at your company's annual meeting, or you are featured in a press conference at which your sales division introduces a new product —all nonthreatening situations.

What may surprise you is that, whether the format is tender or tough, the techniques used in successfully wending your way through a television interview are really quite similar. Unless you understand how to handle the encounter, an inept reporter, who never bothered to read your background material, can cause you as much grief as a muckraker. There's a Russian proverb that says, "There is no good answer to a stupid question."

As an introduction to the process of dealing with TV, I want to take you through an actual case I handled. In some respects, it is a blend of the easy and the difficult. The easy part was that the client really had nothing to hide; the difficult part was that "20/20" and Geraldo Rivera thought it did. Furthermore, Rivera and the program seek headlines. Good news rarely creates them.

Rivera originally established his reputation as a hard-nosed investigative reporter about a decade ago. The exposé that served as his launching pad dealt with New York State's shabby treatment of its mentally retarded citizens. Specifically, Rivera spotlighted Willowbrook, a state hospital on Staten Island in New York City. His cameras focused on the ugliness of the institution, and on such gross examples of maltreatment or outright neglect as residents roaming the halls naked, banging their heads against walls, or lying in their own excrement.

Understandably, the report created a scandal. It led to court suits and a consent decree under which the state agreed to increase dramatically the funding of its programs for the mentally retarded and to make radical changes in methods of treatment and supervision. Under the court's watchful eye, a clean-up, fix-up program was begun. Facilities were upgraded, and deinstitutionalization (the housing of patients in small community residences as opposed to giant "warehouses") became the basic method of domiciling the mentally retarded. New York State spent huge sums in the effort. In fact, the budget of its Office of Mental Retardation and Developmental Disability now totals about $1 billion annually.

I first became involved with the activities of OMRDD because of that quirk in the American psyche that favors progressive programs—until they move in next door. In New York, few neighborhoods were overjoyed at the prospect of harboring a residence occupied by retarded people. OMRDD asked me to conduct a series of workshops aimed at training department representatives on how to conduct themselves when they participated in what were often stormy community meetings.

To get a feeling for the activities of the department, I took guided tours through the institutions, chatted with staff employees, and read through both the consent decree and reams of press clippings. I concluded that, given the immensity of the task it confronted, New York had done a remarkable job of moving into the vanguard of the treatment of the handicapped, even by today's tougher standards.

Understand the weight of the burden. Although overcrowding could be reduced at ancient buildings, some of the buildings still remain in use. Program activities were broadened, but the most severely disabled have such fundamentally crippling limitations that only peripheral changes really take place in their daily existence.

To the untutored eye, especially that of a cameraperson trying to create a riveting documentary, there are scenes within a Willowbrook-type facility that might seem shocking manifestations of negligent care. I can only tell you that, in my judgment, based upon a relationship of several years, OMRDD can be fairly criticized only by those who have worked within the system and understand its limitations. Appreciating the extent of the responsibility is a case of "first walk in my shoes."

In late 1981, OMRDD received notice that Geraldo Rivera and "20/20" planned a follow-up to its initial program, loosely entitled "Willowbrook, Ten Years Later." Department leaders asked me to assist in preparing them for the segment.

Suppose you or your company faced a similar challenge. What preparatory steps should be taken to adequately meet the media?

Here are the questions I ask myself in all cases, and how I go about acting on the answers.

Where Will the Interview Take Place?

If you are invited to a studio, there is nothing that can be done about the setting. Both Don Rickles and you assume the same position on Johnny Carson's couch. However, if the shoot is on site at office or home, your options are considerable. You might deem the appearance of a bustling laboratory preferable to the sterility of a conference room; a talk while walking through the woods might present a more humane picture than the formality of living quarters. Make a decision and then push for that choice. While the press crew will have its own idea of where and what it wants to film, they can be swayed in your direction.

We suggest to clients who habitually deal with the media that they create a pseudotelevision studio in the headquarters building by dressing up one office. The backdrop should be attractive and should include plants or pictures. A sectional couch makes a better seating unit than a desk and chair. Trapped behind the latter, an executive can seem defensive when the reporter leans forward, mike in hand.

Key spokespeople should keep one outfit, suitable for television, permanently in the office closet. Otherwise, it is certain that crew and cameras will arrive on the very day they wear their ugliest, oldest clothes.

In the case of OMRDD, we knew "20/20" would film or tape on site. We speculated about which institutions Rivera and his unit might visit, certain that Willowbrook (now renamed Staten Island Developmental Center) would be one.

I toured potential locations with department members. I suggested a small amount of buffing, polishing, and painting where I thought existing conditions would look shabby on camera. Old window shades were replaced by new ones, lighting wattage increased, and brighter blankets purchased to replace perfectly fine but drab-looking covers.

It is legitimate for you to raise here a fundamental philosophical question. *Is it ethical to make improvements or alterations for the sake of the television camera?*

My response is twofold. First, and very important, these improvements were already scheduled. We simply cut through red tape and expedited delivery. Second, I personally see nothing wrong with putting on your best face when company comes to call.

Recently, a local television show scheduled an interview with a lawyer friend of mine. It was a "happy news" story, focusing on a large judgment he had won in a negligence case. Understandably, the lawyer reacted to the television opportunity with anticipation and excitement. I had to smile at the uncanny "coincidence" that new furniture and modern prints just happened to be on order and suddenly appeared in his office.

There was no deception in the new decor. The lawyer simply wanted his office to look its best. Isn't that exactly the way we all behave when the parents of our child's prospective spouse are to arrive for a first dinner meeting? Isn't that why we put on our best clothing and makeup when dressing for a party?

When "20/20" aired its piece on OMRDD, Rivera made a big fuss over the cosmetic changes at some of the buildings. (He had learned about them from a department employee.) Hugh Downs, host of the program, expressed bewilderment over Rivera's self-righteousness. "What's wrong with trying to make the place look good?" he asked. "It's all part of a massive coverup," Rivera responded.

Poppycock! I take personal responsibility for suggesting the changes, and I did so because I know that isolated dark spots at any location are what an experienced muckraker searches out to make a predetermined point. I wanted to minimize Rivera's opportunities.

Many neophytes suffer damage at the hands of reporters because they treat the experience as if it were a confessional. People who in their private lives exercise their right to compose circumspect answers to a stranger's questions, unaccountably feel a kind of moral and ethical obligation to let everything show on TV.

Keep in mind, please, that meeting Geraldo Rivera or any other journalist is not the same as conversing with a deity. In any TV report, only part of a story can ever be told. It is the right of the subject, *you,* to present your own version in your own way within the boundaries of basic honesty. That is the advice an attorney would give you prior to your testifying in a trial. That is the same standard CBS News applies when it uses makeup on Dan Rather, designs a handsome set for him, and provides a teleprompter so he can read without looking down at a script.

This may be a good place to summarize the outcome of the "20/20" case.

Rivera's conduct, while covering the story, met our expectations. OMRDD's staff was unable to learn in advance, from him or his production assistants, whom he wished to interview, when, or the topics he wished to cover. He chose to arrive at a state institution with camera crew at 5:00 A.M., not exactly an hour when any home is operating at its most efficient. His interviews aimed, in our judgment, less at providing balanced information than at dramatizing his personal crusade.

The end result: Rivera's report ran on two successive programs in twenty-minute segments and revealed nothing untoward in the department's care of its clients—which is why Rivera concentrated on the alleged "repair coverup." Overall content, if not tone, was favorable, as it had to be based upon OMRDD's careful preparation for the interviews and, more important, the fine job the department has done in the years since the consent decree. OMRDD received not one letter or phone call of complaint about department treatment or standards following the programs.

Now lets continue with our checklist of questions to be asked and acted upon before undergoing an appearance on television news.

Who Will Do the Interview?

1.　Always try to learn in advance who actually will conduct the interview. Then check out the reporter on the air. Get a sense of whether his/her style is belligerent or placid.

2.　Does the correspondent seem more interested in eliciting information or making a statement? At the very least, this familiarization will better prepare you for the interloper.

3. Studio interviews are brief—ten to twenty minutes at the most. Interviews, to be edited later, will run on and on if you let them. Don't! Establish ground rules. Set a time limit on the interview—thirty minutes maximum. You have no obligation to permit endless cross-examination. Insist on the right of occasional intermissions, and take them whether needed or not.

What Questions Are Likely to Be Asked?

When I first began consulting with clients on media appearances, I remember being shocked at how little idea they had of what information a reporter would seek in the interview. The naivete seemed incredible until I realized that, unless a person has had the journalistic experience of producing hundreds of stories, the formula element of the procedure is a mystery. And a formula it is.

A professional correspondent can be given research material on a particular story and instantly conjure the three questions he is most likely to ask. On top of those three, perhaps seven other areas of inquiry are pertinent. Thereafter, depending upon how complex the piece is, the next ten questions will aim at flushing out unexpected information. Because it is a formula, if two reporters are assigned to the same story at the same time, you can be almost certain that 90 percent of the questions they ask will be identical.

The trick then is to attempt to anticipate the questions a reporter will ask. Try to put yourself in the reporter's place and think the way he or she would. Don't shy away from the difficult areas. Sometimes, we pretend that maybe if *we* don't think about the sensitive subject, the reporter won't either.

Once, playing interrogator while training the president of a chemical company to respond to attacks about the safety of his plant, I badgered, "How much insurance do you carry to protect the public in event of a disaster?"

My student looked me in the eye and said, "I won't tell you."

Confounded, I dropped my playacting. "You won't what?"

"It is none of the public's business," he answered.

I had to convince him that good preparation demands acceptable answers to likely questions, regardless of how unpalatable they seem. His response wouldn't work on TV and would actually be damaging to him and his company.

Have Answers Been Carefully Prepared?

There is a vast gulf between knowing your business and knowing how to answer questions about it. You can test this thesis quickly by answering these:

1. How large were your company's sales and profits last year? Why were they up or down?

2. How many employees does the firm have?

3. What is the organization's basic line of endeavor—its products and services?

4. What percentage of total revenues did each business segment produce?

5. Who are your main competitors and how do their operations differ from yours?

6. If you were to look five years down the line, what would you expect your company's prospects to be?

7. What is the long-range future of the industry?

If your reaction is typical, you stumbled in two ways. First, you probably had difficulty answering with concrete numbers. In our daily work, most of us can't see the forest for the trees. We can provide the sales figures of our division, but we lose sight of current results in the rest of the company or industry.

Next, you probably rambled in your attempts to answer philosophical questions. Thoughtful people spend much time analyzing their future within a company or where the company itself is heading. But these thoughts do not necessarily translate into a clearly defined total picture that an observer or interviewer would immediately recognize and understand.

With sufficient time and preparation, it is easy to deliver cogent, coherent responses. But without advance planning, choosing the proper language and organization of a reply is difficult. Attempting to deal with questions in an ad-hoc fashion may result in the impression that you don't quite have a grasp of your job or operation.

A news interview can magnify this sense of ineptitude. Reporters and equipment inevitably produce some degree of intimidation and discomfort. If you stumbled a bit answering the questions I posed above while relaxed and in the privacy of your own home, imagine the hurdles you will face when you become conscious that a TV audience is watching.

The prepackaged method of answering questions in a media interview is a classic example of the *illusion* that must be practiced in managing public communication. The effect you should always convey to an audience is that you are delivering replies extemporaneously. In reality, every time you are asked a question, your brain automatically must signal, "Answer 23A" or "Answer 14B."

To accomplish this, don't settle for composing potential answers in your head. Practice speaking them aloud, preferably into a tape recorder. President Reagan dress-rehearses in the White House family theater before every televised press conference, fielding questions tossed at him by staff. The president also prepares thematic points he wants to drive home to the nationwide audience.

What Information Do We Wish to Convey?

The purpose of engaging in a television interview is to meet your own needs, not the reporter's. If you just react to questions, it is likely that your own message will get lost in the dialogue. Set up a clear agenda of the three main points you hope to make. Hammer them home as often as possible during the interview. Sometimes you can use a reporter's question to dovetail into your own area of interest. Other situations may require you to reach out a bit to accomplish that result.

To get a sense of this, take a look at the way politicians handle press questions. They are masters at twisting and turning inquiries to their own advantage. Don't be heavy-handed about this. Over-use of the practice can create an impression of rudeness or lack of candor. But never forget that a press interview, while appearing to be a conversation, is more like an adversarial relationship. You want to score points for yourself, not for the reporter.

The American Way

Europe has its own crew of "image doctors" who work with executives in such countries as Great Britain, France, and Germany. Reading over literature published by some of the more prominent coaches, I was taken by the similarities, but also the differences, in the advice they offer compared to our counsel here in the States. The disparity is most noticeable when it comes to techniques for handling television news interviews. Here are a few examples of contrasting suggestions to amuse you and, perhaps, make you wish your operated over there instead of here.

Abroad: Before the taping, have a thorough workout with the reporter on the subject under discussion and the possible range of questions.

Here: Good luck with that one. OMRDD's inability to obtain a smidgen of advance information from "20/20" typifies the practice of network or major-market reporters here, who consider surprise an effective weapon in the quest for "truth."

Abroad: Discuss with the reporter which segment of the tape you wish to appear on the air and which you prefer to be left on the cutting-room floor.

Here: Such a suggestion would be viewed by our press as an infringement of First Amendment rights—even if the reporter might benefit from knowing which answers would provide the most accurate information.

Abroad: If the interview seems to you unsatisfactory, ask for another one to be taped.

Here: It might be easier to arrange for a winning lottery ticket, especially if you said the wrong thing at the wrong time during the first taping.

Television journalism in the United States is faster, flashier, rougher, and tougher than that abroad. If you wish to utilize the medium successfully, you must engage in combat according to the rules of the battlefield. I can provide you a historical analogy.

During the opening stages of our Revolutionary War, the Redcoats behaved like civilized soldiers. They would approach battle on the village green in perfect formation; the frontline would drop to its knees, fire a uniform round of shots, and then exit as the next line took its place. There was one little problem: the British were getting slaughtered by rebel forces who wore camouflaged clothing, shot from behind trees, and then disappeared before the enemy could draw a bead on them. In other words, the Redcoats fought according to the rules; the Americans fought to win.

Whenever you feel that the strategems required to meet the American press on its own terms seem unsportsmanlike, I suggest you remind yourself that you live in the United States of America and not a British colony. That reminder should serve to assure you to fight fire with fire if you want to win the TV wars.

13 When the Red Light Is On

I'm convinced that the attention span of Americans is diminishing. No one today sits voluntarily through a two-hour speech; few wade through the detail of a Charles Dickens novel. We expect information to be offered to us in a fast, painless way, enlivened with dynamics, graphics, and dramatics.

I suspect that television has had much to do with this national inability to sit still and concentrate. When "Sesame Street" introduces education to four-year-old children in rapid bursts of visual and vocal pyrotechnics, it is reasonable to conclude that more than content is being taught. When complicated stories are presented by news programs in only ninety seconds, is the short time span just a reflection of our frenetic way of life or a case of TV making us frenetic? It doesn't require a great imagination to contemplate a future when communication will take place in the atmosphere of an old Mack Sennett movie—jerky images of people jumping up and down, delivering and receiving only the tiniest bits and pieces of knowledge without time for in-depth examination or insight.

As a professional communicator, I deal with reality as I find it, and I counsel my clients to do the same. Speeches must be brief; appearances on television geared to an even briefer span.

Television is a headline medium. Depth and detail are tough to get across because the medium operates within strict time constraints. In his 1982 book *Newswatch: How TV Decides the News,* (Simon & Schuster) veteran producer Av Westin of ABC acknowledges the almost obsessive concern TV people have with the clock. Programs, commercials, and correspondent news reports must start on time and end on time. Otherwise the whole system falls apart.

Westin relates an amusing story about Fred Friendly, when he was president of CBS News. A producer mistakenly ended a program two minutes early. To fill the time before the next scheduled broadcast, credits rolled across the screen at a tortoise pace. Infuriated, Friendly ripped his expensive watch off his wrist and handed it to the chagrined producer. "Here," he said, according to Westin. "Take it. You need it more than I do."

To appreciate this preoccupation with mere seconds, study a program like "TODAY" on NBC-TV. Jane Pauley is interviewing Dr. X about the herpes virus epidemic. Dr. X is full of information but a trifle slow getting to the main point. Just as he warms up, Ms. Pauley breaks in and says, "Thank you very much, doctor—most interesting. We'll be right back after this commercial message." To hell with herpes. A hemorrhoid remedy spot is slotted for 8:09–30. By God it will run at 8:09–30 or else. Priorities must be kept. Herpes is going to be around tomorrow; a missed commercial is lost forever.

A sense of time must affect your every decision when you're on television. Generally, keep your answers about fifteen to twenty seconds in length. That is the maximum used in most news pieces. In taped interviews, it is crucial to aim exactly for fifteen to twenty seconds. If your answers exceed twenty seconds, they will be edited. If they are only five seconds each, three of these bits will be strung together in the editing room. Don't give news people such power. You may not like the end result.

If participating as a guest in a panel program, you can exceed fifteen to twenty seconds, but fight off the temptation to reach for a minute. By television standards, a minute is a lifetime. Not long ago, I attended a public relations conference where a speaker showed a 1950s Eastern Airlines commercial that ran 2 1/2 minutes, It seemed like a documentary.

Make Statements Colorful and Dramatic

Since little time is available for each answer, your choice of words should slant toward the dramatic. Try to get your main point into the opening few lines. That way, if you should be interrupted in midstream, or your answer edited, the basic thrust of the message will survive.

Use the Iceberg Approach

Because businesspeople know their operations from top to bottom, they often say too much when asked about them. Baring your soul to a reporter is like opening Pandora's Box. You may not be able to control the evils that come tumbling out.

One of the oldest interviewing tricks in the book is to stare at a subject you have just intimidated. It is astonishing how long people under stress will talk, literally afraid to stop. Often tasty morsels emerge from the monologue, which the reporter can utilize to pillory the victim even further.

A variation on this theme concerns the interviewee who is emotionally ready to "unload." For underlying personal reasons, the individual wants to confide. To avoid this catastrophe, always prepare answers in the "iceberg" fashion. The first reply to any inquiry is the simplest one that meets the need. It is the above-the-water-line answer. Then stop. If the reporter requests more information, have a level-B answer ready—one that goes ten feet beneath the water line. Stop again. Only submerge to the ocean floor with information when absolutely necessary.

Make a Give

No one is perfect! I remind you of the cliché because often we ignore it, to our detriment. There is nothing less credible than the executive who goes before the public and defends every company action, no matter how clearly in error. People make mistakes; companies make mistakes. If you can look directly into the camera and say, where justified, "We blew that one," you will help your cause immeasurably.

I don't expect you to reveal every blemish and wart in your operation. To the contrary, I have already stressed that a television interview is the wrong place to seek the philosophical essence of truth and goodness. There are two sides to every story. Seek penance in another forum. What I am suggesting is that where you can "make a give" that costs your cause very little, make it.

If your company has settled out of court a suit alleging sexual discrimination in hiring and promotion, there are two ways to deal with a reporter's question about such unlawful practices. Answer A fights off the accusation with indignation and the lame defense that the settlement aimed only at avoiding protacted litigation. Answer B, infinitely better, faces the issue squarely: "Most corporations in this country have been slow to recognize the legitimate rights of women in the workplace, and I think we were equally sluggish. The suit spurred us in the right direction, and I can assure you we are moving forward as rapidly as possible to correct inequities."

Such a reply costs you or your firm nothing. Once you settled that suit, the rabbit escaped from the hat. Bid it goodbye with graciousness rather than meanness of spirit.

Stick to Your Own Line

Ask us a question, and most of us will answer—whether we know much about the subject or not. In a television news interview, such an exhibition of ego can hurt you. I prove this to clients in the oil industry during practice training sessions by suddenly switching from questions about oil to inquiries about nuclear energy. "Do

you believe that nuclear power has a role in our energy future?"
I ask. "Absolutely," comes the answer. "Nuclear power must be
part of our energy mix." Having goaded the client into a response
like that, I then run through a nasty series of questions about
nuclear safety, cost overruns, etc. The video playback helps me
make the point. "Don't you have enough problems dealing with
oil issues without trying to be an expert about nuclear power,
too?"

You have a right—even a duty—to answer questions only about
your own field. Don't be trapped into skating onto thin ice that
may break and plunge you into cold waters.

Evading Questions

A common thread running through my conversations with clients
is: "How do I evade questions I don't want to answer?" To me, this
question indicates a troublesome mind set. Your basic policy in
confronting the media should concentrate on the method of preparing for questions, not evading them. Ninety-nine percent of a
successful television appearance is directly related to the effort
you put in before the action begins. Do your homework adequately, and bobbing, weaving, and ducking questions will be
unnecessary.

But there *are* dodges that can be ethically used.

Before replying to a complicated query about an unpleasant
topic, ask that the question be repeated or more fully explained.
The ten seconds of breather space this gives you offers an opportunity to mentally place your cards in the proper order before dealing them.

Similarly, practice brushing negative topics quickly off the ta-
bletop and elaborate upon every morsel of good news. So, if asked
about the "sex discrimination" case, acknowledge it with a brief
reply and move on. If asked about an upturn in profits, dwell on
it lovingly and at length.

If you don't know an answer, say, "I don't know." Don't adopt
a posture of omnipotent wisdom. Even if you have some slight
knowledge of an incident you don't wish to discuss, say, "I don't

know." Facing a camera is not so different from occupying the witness chair in open court. Don't ever lie. I stress that: *Don't ever lie!* But don't feel morally obligated to tell more than you have to or would be expected to. You don't have to incriminate yourself and you just might if you babble on with little or no self-control and with a great deal of dangerous ignorance.

Stay Cool

Do not get personally involved in the give and take of an interview. Aggressive reporters like nothing better than rattling an interviewee, because anger often causes us to say the wrong things in the wrong way.

I had a reputation for being a tough television questioner. Often, following a program, a tormented guest would wail, "You were so nice when we had coffee before the show." I would point out that I might be equally pleasant company at lunch later, but once that red light went on, business is business. To the reporter, any interview is one more job. Try to adopt the same workmanlike attitude.

Play a Role!

The audience will remember little of what you had to say in a television segment but a great deal about you. I discussed the reasons at length in the chapter on *images.* Be certain before you walk onto a set that you have determined the impressions you wish to leave behind. Make sure your words and actions accentuate this *image.*

Stay Conversational

Millions of people may watch a television program, but the viewing is a private experience, shared at most with just a few companions.

Author Marshall McLuhan labeled the medium "cool," meaning

that its format meshed best with a laid-back approach. I prefer to use the word *intimate*. We are closely involved with the image on the screen. If that image is too overbearing, we become exhausted. There is too little space to absorb the outpouring of energy. Easygoing personalities wear well and have long careers on television; those who are acerbic or overwhelming soon wear out their welcome.

When on the tube, stay conversational. Do not overuse facial expressions. If you frown or laugh too broadly, a tight camera shot will make you appear a gargoyle. As I described earlier, determining an acceptable scope of facial expression requires careful fine-tuning. Practicing on videotape is most helpful in learning the distinction between what is too understated and what is excessive.

In Chapter 10, I noted that the television medium, properly utilized, can be a powerful tool in helping individuals and institutions reach out to the public. Before concluding this part of the book, I want to make you aware of the most common method of obtaining access to television news time and how to go about taking advantage of it.

The Press Conference

To a major organization, the process of holding a press conference is routine. To the individual, small company, or trade association, the challenge is bewildering, presenting an array of problems to be solved and decisions to be made. The following advice may be of benefit to the sophisticated in this area, but I hope it will be especially helpful to the small budget operation.

The first requirement for anyone holding a press conference is to assure yourself an audience. If your firm is embroiled in a crisis, it is easy to entice the media to your meeting. Without formal invitation, they will arrive en masse. But if your subject matter is noncontroversial, making an offer that can't be refused requires imagination. Keep sight of the fact that media journalists have a market just as you do. An editor's task is to fill air time with stories that capture viewers. If you are to attain media exposure, your story and media needs must converge.

To assure adequate attendance at your conference, send out an advisory to the assignment editors at the TV (or radio) stations important to you. Make it brief and include basics such as time, place, the name of a contact source within your organization, video opportunities, and, of course, a "hook" telling why the information to be presented will be of interest to viewers.

The day before the session, telephone the people to whom you sent advisories. Remind them of the meeting, and try to convince them of its importance. The telephone call followup is essential. Media news people are inundated with releases on every subject from the local flower show to the plumbers' convention. If your call comes in on a day when newsworthy stories are few, you have a decent chance of making it onto the home screen that night.

Choose a room which will comfortably accommodate thirty to forty people, making certain it is equipped with enough electrical outlets and power. Try to develop posters or other backdrops for TV crews to shoot. Graphically dramatic slides or charts are helpful. Be sure to book a separate, smaller room for individual interviews.

For television, the conference must be strategically timed. Hold it as early in the day as possible, enabling reporters to have plenty of editing time before the 6:00 P.M. newscast. Aim for the middle or end of the week. As the weekend approaches, the number of major stories often dwindle, making your "soft" piece more desirable.

On the day of the meeting, have a press kit available. This package includes a more detailed news release, a copy of key statements made at the conference, and other brochures or background information. Have coffee and doughnuts available as well. A well-fed reporter is a kindlier reporter.

Allow scheduling leeway to meet the needs of late-arriving crews; be prepared to repeat statements, if necessary, just for them. Don't be uptight about this. It is part of the *illusion* of television. Also, don't be disconcerted by reporters coming and going during the course of the meeting. Crews often cover several stories in a morning so they shoot the essentials of one and then rush off to the next. After the conference is completed, check your list of names invited and call those who failed to attend. Make a spokesperson available for interviews later in the day by those who missed the main event.

Of course, follow all the other procedures detailed in this section. Plan your answers, have spokespeople who project vitality, and create your own headlines. Don't expect to be 100 percent successful. If 80 percent of the broadcast story meets your needs, that's probably a better batting average than you have in your own business or profession.

PART FIVE

From the Rostrum

14 Drafting Material That Works

Like a bus driver who enjoys motoring during holidays, my avocation is watching other speakers at work. With no professional obligations, I can relax and, I hope, just enjoy the speaker. Besides, there is a bonus. I almost always learn something new. Sometimes the lesson is positive: I discover a clever approach to the audience or a bit of witty material I can adapt for my own purposes. But equally instructive is witnessing the communication exercise that fails. What mistakes were made? Where did the speaker go wrong? How do I avoid similar errors by myself or clients? George Burns once remarked that long after his wife, Gracie Allen, became a featured performer, she still used to study other acts in progress. When another's routine played poorly, she would say to Burns, "George, remind me never to do that on stage." You can benefit from a similar critical approach. Instead of just watching other communicators, begin to analyze what they do and how they do it. It will help refine your own skills.

That's what the next several chapters are about, refining your speechmaking skills. You will find many practical tips on how to improve everything from drafting material to choosing a style of delivery. Absorb this information in the context of producing *a total public appearance*. A total public appearance begins when you conceptualize what you hope to accomplish, labor long and hard over the substance of your message, extensively practice delivery, assure that your stage has been set for maximum impact, and, finally, understand audience-control techniques. Let's take the process step by step.

Getting the Material Together

There is a wonderful anecdote, perhaps apocryphal, about the late Jack Benny. A nonperforming colleague kept needling the comedian that with first-class material even an amateur could be funny. Benny took the abuse for a while, then suggested the acquaintance sit through a specific show. On the prescribed evening, Benny strode on stage, carrying a copy of the local telephone directory. In the halting style and with the timing that kept him a star over four decades, he began to slowly read a list of names. Within seconds, the audience convulsed with laughter.

That kind of talent made Jack Benny unique. Nevertheless, throughout his long, successful career, Benny kept a stable of expensive comedy writers on payroll. He knew that no matter how engaging the personality or how dynamic the style, great presentations begin with well-constructed material.

When I work on a specific presentation with a client, I usually videotape a first reading. Occasionally, after listening for five minutes to a jumble of unconnected facts and observations, I interrupt by exclaiming, "Hold it! What are you trying to get at? You have no clear direction."

Developing material that works is somewhat like cutting a path through a forest. You must have a clear idea of your ultimate destination, an imaginative yet definite route marked out for getting there, a compass to keep you on track, and a willingness to hack away at obstructions. A speaker must meet similar standards —focusing on the ultimate goal of the remarks, striving for lively, colorful language, sticking to the basic themes en route, and editing out all unnecessary words and phrases that clutter the message and distract from impact.

Shaping ideas into a coherent, cohesive, informative, and entertaining pattern is an art. Since few people are gifted with natural creative ability, hard work has to substitute for genius.

The famed sports columnist Red Smith, when asked the secret of his ability to turn out consistently marvelous prose, replied, "It's easy. I just sit at the typewriter until beads of blood break out on my forehead."

Professional speechwriters labor for many hours on a single major address. They write, rewrite, and then write some more. The harder your effort, the more satisfactory the result. The trick is not to let your hard work show; the speech should come across as a relaxed, almost impromptu experience for the listener. The task is less fearsome then you might imagine.

What to Talk About

In either the work environment or a social setting, subject matter evolves from your expertise. Henry Kissinger lectures about foreign affairs; Rona Barrett gossips about Hollywood; you are called upon to speak about your own specialty. Both in drafting a speech and delivering it, this restriction is an asset rather than a liability. I will explain why shortly.

When you decide which concepts are worth exploring, the next step is to just think for a while. Amateurs have a tendency to rush the writing process. A brainstorm explodes and there is an immediate rush to set it down on paper. Often the idea that seemed so golden appears tarnished upon lengthier consideration.

It is much wiser to allow the inspiration to jell over several days. Play with it mentally, get a feeling of whether it has substance or is paper thin. Then, perhaps while going to and from work, test your thoughts by saying them aloud. Hearing what your ideas sound like may reveal some false notes in their organization and expression.

Once you've played around with your subject, your next step is to flesh out the framework. Attention to detail often makes the difference between a mundane speech and a magnificent one. Years ago, I interviewed the crime story author of *The Friends of Eddie Coyle,* George Higgins. He commented that his writing technique involved a heavy use of detail. By that he meant that instead of referring to a pistol, he carefully describes the texture of the weapon—a Smith & Wesson .45 caliber with a wooden handle, scratched barrel, etc. The idea is to create a clear picture in the reader's mind. Good speech material strives for the same goals.

Anecdotes, quotes, and philosophical references are essential seasonings. Start a collection in your file cabinet. Keep clippings from newspapers and magazines, old speeches, copies of others' speeches, jokes, and any other kind of source material that might be useful. After all, to create a new speech from scratch each time the podium beckons is a monumental task. It is easier and more fruitful to redesign and retailor already existing material. Stealing material word for word is illegal, but borrowing and adapting ideas is neither plagaristic nor unethical.

The First Draft

There are two ways of drafting speech material. One is to write or type the contents. The shortcomings of this method are a speech full of awkward phrases, sentences that are too long, or language that is too flowery. We fall into this trap because our experience of writing is mostly that which is meant for reading, not writing created for speaking aloud. Each style involves different skills.

To compensate, I suggest you first arrange your thoughts and jot down notes about them on a pad. Next, using the notes to stay on track, ramble through the speech, recording the effort with a tape recorder or dictaphone. Ignore stumbling and repetition. Just keep going until completion. Transcribe this rough version. Then begin editing and refining until a usable speech emerges. Vocabulary will be more colloquial, words easier to pronounce, and sentences shorter and more declarative. Furthermore, the process is faster.

How Long Should a Speech Be?

This is one of those questions equivalent to how many angels can fit on the head of a pin. One of the common answers is that a speech should be like a woman's skirt—long enough to cover the subject and short enough to make it interesting. An amusing quip, but absolutely useless for our purpose.

Here's a more helpful guideline. In today's rapidly paced environment, a typical address to a typical audience should run fifteen to twenty minutes, with perhaps a maximum of ten additional minutes allotted for questions. Now, I know you can rightfully challenge me with many exceptions. What about the situations where your role is merely to introduce the keynoter? What about the boss, who insists you present a forty-five-minute report? What about . . . ? When the "what abouts" are the dominant factor, adjust accordingly. But for the *typical speech* to the *typical audience,* fifteen to twenty minutes is about right.

A speech five to ten minutes long barely allows an audience to make your acquaintance. A speech greater than thirty minutes requires brilliant material and a super style of delivery to retain attention. Even then the chances are excellent that listener attention will drift.

I once introduced the columnist Jack Anderson to a gathering in Baltimore. Anderson had often guested on talk shows I hosted. He is an excellent speaker. But on this occasion he rambled on for nearly an hour. Twenty-five minutes into the presentation, I felt the audience begin to wander. Thirty-five minutes on the clock and he got them back. Forty-five minutes and they were gone again. Anderson's comments were well received, but in my judgment he could have been even more effective by shortening his speech.

Remember the story about Lincoln, who said that it took him two weeks to prepare a twenty-minute speech, one week to shape a forty-minute speech, and that he could do an hour off the top of his head? It's easy to be longwinded and redundant; the challenge is to communicate the message in a streamlined fashion.

Clues to a Vibrant, Fast-Moving Speech

Make sure your speech has a strong beginning and conclusion. There is a theatrical adage that a show with a good first act and a good third act can survive a weak second act. So it is with a speech. Start dramatically and finish dramatically. Put the technical material in the middle.

Good openings and closings are limited only by imagination. They can be humorous, motivational, or hint at great things ahead. What they should not offer is a chronological recitation. There is nothing more tedious than speech or conversation that monotonously goes from A to Z. Build mystery into your material so the audience has to keep awake if it wants the secrets ahead.

Here is a condensed example of a good teasing opening.

> A lot of people ask me how I do it. After all, twenty-two is a pretty young age to be the top widget salesman in the Northeast. It wasn't easy when I started out. I had trouble getting the fat cats to even meet with me. Those men are busy guys. They've got a lot of years of experience, and they expect to deal with seasoned professionals. I had to make up for my lack of years somehow. It was either dye my hair gray or come up with a plan. Well, I came up with a plan, one that can work for you too.
>
> I knew that, once I got in the door, I had the wherewithal to impress purchasing execs and CEOs. My product was first rate. *Consumer Complaints* had ranked our widgets number one for the past six years. My company had been around for years, was very solid, and had a history free of inventory problems. What we promised, we delivered. Only one delivery over one gross had been delivered past deadline in twenty-three years . . . and that was during the truckers' strike. Our price had been consistently competitive, and still is. Then, as now, there was no reason not to buy from Wizard Widget.
>
> All I had to do was get that first appointment. That's where my plan came in handy. Now, it's not an easy plan. It requires true stick-to-itiveness. But, sooner or later, it always gets me in that door. "So, what is this brilliant strategy?" you're probably asking yourselves.

The opening now leads into the body of the address:

> *I refused to take no for an answer.* If I was told Mr. Smith couldn't see me on a Tuesday, I went back to see him on Wednesday, and if need be, Thursday, Friday, Saturday, and Sunday. After a while,

> Mr. Smith would get used to seeing me around and it would occur
> to him that he wasn't going to get rid of me until he gave me some
> time. Now I won't say that I've sold widgets to every person I
> pitched to. At least not yet.

And a closing:

> So that's my plan. I suggest you fledgling salespeople try it out for
> size. Never take no for an answer . . . and remember, you have the
> best-quality product at the lowest price in the area: the Wizard
> Widget.

Once having chosen your basic themes, concentrate on them.
Don't try to accomplish too much in any one speech. Constantly
branching off with subheadings and digressions causes confusion
and loss of interest. In oral communication, limited objectives lead
to better results.

Be careful about use of statistics. Too many make the head
swim. Utilize visual supports if you have to present many numbers. More on visuals shortly.

*Make certain your use of language creates a series of "gee
whizzes."* In other words, listeners should be saying to themselves,
"Gee whiz, I didn't know that." Or, "Gee whiz, how about that?"
Material aimed at the gut tends to be more impressive than ab-
stract intellectual concepts.

For example, I have worked extensively with the oil industry.
One question repeatedly hurled at industry officials had to do with
nationalization. Instead of replying with a lengthy philosophical
explanation of the disadvantages of government ownership and
management, oil executives were counseled to use this reply: "If
you like the Federal Post Office, you'll love nationalized oil." What
the answer accomplished was an immediate image of how ineffec-
tively the government operates the businesses it is already in.

*Keep sentences short, usually fewer than twenty words. Vary
length to avoid monotony.*

Keep the language itself easy to comprehend. The old acronym
is still a good one—KISS: Keep It Simple, Stupid. Don't permit ego

or carelessness to thwart simplicity. Ego demands that we appear highly learned by utilizing a large, complex vocabulary. Unfortunately, few listeners will absorb our message.

Complex: "For years, I have considered the only instrument capable of bestowing upon me connubial bliss. I beg of you to join hands with me in matrimony."

Simple: "Marry me, please."

Complex: "It has come to my attention that your township may have a position for which one with my experience and expertise might be appropriate. Even though I am not acquainted with hook-and-ladder apparatus or carbon tetrachloride, I do consider myself a foe of combustion, an enemy of smotheration, and a man of expeditious action. Also, it would behoove you to consider my past performance in this country's armed military forces, one signalized by a propensity for self-aggrandizement achieved by conspicuous deeds."

Simple: "I am interested in the job of fireman that you have posted. Although I do not have a background in fire fighting, I believe my military history, as well as my desire to protect the community from fire or any other hazard, qualifies me for consideration."

Carelessness involves overusing professional terminology and inside references. Attorneys are prime offenders, but they have no monopoly on the market. To outsiders, shorthand expressions are gobbledygook, every bit as indecipherable as an exotic foreign language.

Be careless and you risk using expressions that have become red flag items—or are hopelessly out of date. Calling women "gals" or talking about corporate responsibility are examples. Heartfelt though the sentiment may be when a businessperson refers to "corporate responsibility," the phrase is met with considerable skepticism.

A slogan of ancient vintage is: "No one ever went broke underestimating the intelligence of the American people." A variation is: "No one ever communicates less by constantly simplifying and updating material."

The necessity to edit, reedit, and then edit some more cannot be overstressed. Consider this sentence: "In conclusion, ladies and gentlemen, I urge you to remember that America the Beautiful has achieved the summit of power and respect not by shirking its responsibilities, not by failing to bite the bullet, but by taking the reins of industrialism firmly in hand and steering a clear, aggressive path down the track."

Before reading further, stop and consider how you might get across a similar theme more effectively.

My own suggestions (and they constitute *an* approach, not *the* approach) are: The sentence is too long to be expressed aloud easily. Although bombastic language may have its place very occasionally, cliches and mixed metaphors always overwhelm the underlying thrust. The statement works better when simplified: "In conclusion, remember this country achieved power and respect by moving aggressively toward chosen goals. We cannot shirk our responsibilities. We must get back on the industrial track."

When editing, allow gaps of time from one session to another. Give your brain a chance to clear, encouraging reevaluation with a constantly fresh perspective. *However,* always draw a line beyond which you make no further text changes. Making adjustments right to the moment when you begin speaking is a fundamental error. Delivery will suffer from either the insecurity caused by trying to recall last-minute alterations or from struggling to read scribbled inserts and deletions. Like a production trying out on Broadway, there is a time to "lock in" what you have and go with it.

Try to incorporate humor. There are few experiences so tedious as being lectured to without respite. Podium professionals always leaven their remarks with a steady supply of quips and anecdotes. Developing and polishing this material is hard work, but the payoff is worth the effort.

Why Is It Tough for Amateur Comedians to Get a Laugh?

Conditioning

A basic consideration underlying successful humor is the more conditioned an audience is to laugh, the funnier the comic routine! An old Bob Hope radio script illustrates the point. In the routine,

Hope is accosted by a robber who demands: "Your money or your life." There is a long pause. Forcefully, the thief repeats the threat: "Your money or your life." After another agonizing silence, Hope responds, "I'm thinking about it."

An amusing bit, you will agree, but no blockbuster. Indeed, Hope never did the skit. Jack Benny did. Now it takes on a different dimension. Given Benny's carefully developed character as a tightwad, the pauses and punchline become hilarious. The sequence produced one of the longest sustained roars of amusement in the history of radio comedy. That's what I mean by conditioning. Audiences were primed to laugh at anything involving Benny's parsimony.

The amateur comedian faces a self-evident problem. There is no track record preparing an audience to laugh at the jokes of a vice-president of finance suddenly cast in the role of a stand-up comic.

Material

Star comics hire expensive writers. That's a luxury we can't afford, so we settle instead for retelling the joke heard last week at the office or neighborhood bar. Unfortunately, everyone in our audience heard it last week—or even last year—as well. For example, any speaker who begins his address with this story should be throttled: "In deciding what to say to you, I feel a little bit like Elizabeth Taylor's last husband on their honeymoon. I know what has to be done, but I'm not sure how to make it interesting."

Without exaggerating, I have heard that line delivered from the rostrum by amateur comics a minimum of one hundred times. It is so old that the barb was directed originally at Zsa Zsa Gabor. Still, people tell this hoary relic as if it were created yesterday.

Execution

Successfully telling a good tale requires courage that amateurs lack. Instead, they start a joke and then begin to doubt themselves during the rendition. The mind teases—I'll bet they've heard it before . . . or I'll bet they are a bunch of sobersides who won't laugh. Panic sets in and inexperienced humorists swallow or rush the punchline, guaranteeing the fiasco they dreaded. I witnessed one embarrassing incident when the speaker took two minutes to set up his punchline and then forgot it. The audience sat stunned, unsure whether to laugh politely in support of the speaker or raucously at his discomfiture.

How Can These Difficulties Be Overcome?

Avoid Joke Jokes.

Instead, find anecdotes that can be adapted to appear real. For example, a utility official might do well with this one: "I work in a crazy business. Last week, driving along the highway, I spotted a power grid with a sign reading 'Danger! High Voltage. Do not touch! Anyone who touches will be prosecuted to the fullest extent of the law.'"

Because the jest has a modicum of truth and is related to the speaker's occupation, it does not announce itself in advance as a deliberate attempt at being funny. Like any good investment, we want the highest potential profit for the least amount of capital. Even moderate chuckles are a plus.

Finding jokes to modify requires effort and patience. Spend an afternoon in the library thumbing through old jokebooks. The older, the better. Gags from a 1950s *Readers Digest* may be new to today's listener. Be discriminating. Hours of searching may only turn up a couple of worthwhile tidbits.

Shape every story to match your own phrasing style and sense of timing.

Weed out all unnecessary detail; it weighs jokes down.

Keep anecdotes brief.

Three to four lines are sufficient. Let Bob Newhart do lengthy monologues. That's his business.

Be careful about ethnic and off-color material.

Some of the truest humor is ethnic in origin. But we live in an era of intense cultural awareness and sensitivity. Pat Cooper can kid Italians; Alan King can handle Jewish humor; Richard Pryor can poke fun at blacks; outsiders have no similar charter. Leave that hilarious ethnic joke at home.

I am not quite so dogmatic about off-color humor. Although the safest rule is to shelve it, a double entendre can be effective if in good taste. Real smut and graphic sexual descriptions are, of course, totally unacceptable. But a joke that wittily plays on the peculiarities of human sexuality can be entertaining and an asset to a presentation. Providing, of course, that the audience will be responsive to a risque comment. It's important to know the composition of your audience.

If a joke dies, don't die with it.

Just keep moving forward without apology. If you make a big deal about the flop, it upsets everyone's equilibrium and the momentum of the address.

Remember that good material constitutes 50 percent or more of an effective presentation. Choosing, structuring, and polishing text is a step-by-step process. Don't skip or rush through any part of it. Settling for less than the best, in style and shape of content, guarantees a mediocre result.

Here are some books about speech material, you may find useful: *Braude's Source Book for Speakers and Writers,* by Jacob M. Braude (Englewood Cliffs, NJ: Prentice-Hall, 1968); *How to Make Speeches for All Occasions,* by Harold P. and Marjorie E. Zelko (New York: Doubleday & Co., 1971); *The Successful Speaker's Planning Guide,* by Edward Hegarty (New York: McGraw-Hill, 1970); *Speechwriting: The Master Touch,* by Joseph J. Kelley, Jr. (Harrisburg, PA: Stackpole, 1980); *The Toastmaster's Treasure Chest,* by Herbert V. Prochnow and Herbert V. Prochnow, Jr. (New York: Harper and Row, 1979); and *Podium Humor,* by James C. Humes (New York: Harper and Row, 1975).

15 Developing a Dynamic Style of Delivery

A speech is like an iceberg. To the casual listeners, only the above-the-waterline portion—the delivery—shows. The effort behind the writing, editing, practicing, and setting of the stage is unseen. For purposes of clarity, I want to discuss first the tip of the iceberg —*delivery*. Then we can return to the backstage preparation that precedes it.

There are really only three approaches available to you in the actual delivery of the material: (1) use a prepared text, (2) rely upon notes to support your remarks, or (3) attempt to ad-lib the entire presentation. Is one preferable to the others or are they equally acceptable? Let's examine them individually.

Reading from Text

Reading aloud to an audience is a sure way to put it to sleep. Perhaps some speakers can hold the attention of an audience in this way, but they are members of a very small, very elite tribe.

Oral communication depends upon a shared intimacy between sender and receiver. Intimacy develops from both physical presence and eye contact. Speakers who read their speeches sacrifice both. Because they require a lectern to hold text, they are locked into one position for the duration of the talk. Such a speech is boring to give and to listen to. The audience is isolated from the speaker, standing at a lectern usually ten feet away from the first row and a figurative mile from the last. Intimacy is impossible, and so the audience, forced to remain focused on a static figure, begins to doze. Eye contact falls victim to the "bobbing for apples" syndrome, for as the speaker looks for each line, the head nods up and down repetitively as if searching for fruit in a barrel. The movement becomes monotonous for the speaker and the audience.

Admittedly, there are occasions when reading from a text is appropriate and necessary. For the president of the United States to speak of momentous national policies off-the-cuff is foolhardy and dangerous. Similarly, I can't imagine a utility executive winging it before a rate-setting commission or a personnel director casually commenting on an equal-opportunity lawsuit.

The guideline, then, for when to make your speech from a prepared text is simple and straightforward. In those cases when every word counts, every word read should be written. Otherwise, there are better approaches.

If speaking from a text is called for, there are techniques that can increase its effectiveness. To begin with, try to make the finished script sound as if it were created to be spoken rather than created to be read in a book. It will sound more natural. Next, be sure the material is laid out properly. Margins should be substantial, with the width of the line not much in excess of those shown below:

This is a good width for a line of type on paper.

The idea is to keep the line brief enough to encourage eye absorption of word blocks, which enables the speaker to spend more time looking at the audience and less time locked onto the paper. Notice how easy it is to grasp the contents of the above demonstration sentence with one eye scan.

A good way to practice reading phrases or lines is to speak the following paragraph aloud as you would in a public appearance. Take note of how often you look up and down.

> I am honored that you have elected me mayor of this fine city. I am especially touched because I take this as a vote of confidence, a sign that the people of this city know what I have maintained all along, that my conviction was a sham. And that you know that I can serve as well from prison as my opponents could from City Hall. May the world know what the people of Metropolis know: I am not a crook!

Now try it again. This time, keep your eyes down until you can absorb the four or five words preceding a punctuation mark such as a comma or a period. As soon as the phrase is fixed in your mind, look up for the entire span. Do not drop your eyes again until you have finished the phrase. Overall eye contact will be much greater than with word-by-word reading, which causes more constant head bobbing.

For easier reading, *have the script prepared with all capital letters.* Better yet, utilize the Orator typeface now available on many typewriters and word processors.

"For the practicing physical therapist, the attending physician is a focal point for the further treatment of the patient. In other words, the physical therapist complements the physician's work."

If this is impossible, double-space the lines and quadruple-space paragraphs. Too much print clustered together makes it easy to lose your place when looking up and down.

Use visual punctuation. Try ". . ." in place of a "," for marking a pause. Try "//" rather than a "." to indicate the end of a sentence. See how clearly these marks serve as phrasing instructions.

By all means, underline key words and phrases. Guessing what to emphasize once you're onstage is tough going. Watch out, though, for the trap of overabundant underlining. Students are often prey to this. Look at their textbooks and you will notice whole pages marked up. Underlining a complete page, of course, defeats the whole purpose of underlining. Nothing is marked for emphasis. Think through where the punch lines really belong before marking up your script.

What About Notes?

Ask a sample of one hundred people the technique they prefer in addressing an audience, and ninety-five will respond, "Notes." Ask the same sample why and several explanations emerge. First, notes are comfortable. They alleviate the fear of going blank, a dreadful prospect for an already nervous speaker. Next, they prevent important elements of the message from falling through the cracks of memory, never to be aired.

Ask me how I feel about the use of notes and I answer: *Notes are the worst way to deliver a speech!*

I know that is a bold statement, one that conflicts with much expert opinion. Indeed, a competitor of my firm bases all its instruction on the technique of using a flip chart as a crib sheet. It tells all clients to "touch, turn, and tell." The idea is to disguise the outline headings by placing them in full view on a wall chart. Glancing at the chart for memory reinforcement, the speaker *touches* the next point to be made for emphasis, *turns* to the audience, and then *tells* all about it. It's an interesting gimmick, but a hollow one.

Any device that turns a speaker into a robot diminishes the opportunity and capacity to achieve excellence. Crutches of any type, relied upon on a regular basis—and that's what notes are, a crutch pure and simple—limit the effectiveness and potential of the speaker and the speech. It's comparable to the disabled person who can stand and even walk with the use of a cane. But run at full speed? Never! If you wish to be a first-rate, attention-holding speaker, then notes must be discarded.

Notes permit neither the physical and mental freedom of an

ad-lib presentation, nor the security and stability of prepared text. Observe carefully and you will recognize that note aficionados fall victim to the same failing as those who speak from a prepared text. They rarely wander far from the lectern and busily, monotonously, and repeatedly glance down at the headings beneath them. Why? Because once we know that print exists, we tend to glance obsessively at it, if only to assure ourselves it is still there.

With their "apple bobbing" head movements, note readers remind me of a tic exhibited by many TV anchorpeople. As I indicated earlier, all anchorpeople have two scripts available, one the sheaf of papers on the desk, the other displayed on the teleprompter. No matter where they look, they are reading. The desired illusion is to convince the home audience that the anchorperson has such a complete grasp of the day's events that he or she can look down briefly at the pile of papers and then give the next news story from memory. What really is happening, of course, is that while the anchorperson is looking directly into the camera, the mechanical idiot card is providing information.

Where the game falls apart is that many anchorpeople cannot move easily from reading from the script to reading from the prompter. So what they do is rely totally upon the prompter and look down just for effect. Watch closely and you will be amused at how many of these professionals drop their eyes, but not nearly long enough to absorb any of the material in front of them. It's total fakery. Just as it is when note readers duck their heads; they are searching not for information, but security.

Convincing clients to give up notes is a formidable challenge. When I propose it, the reaction is unbridled panic. One woman looked at me wide-eyed and exclaimed, "Without notes, I think I'd vomit." Extreme, yes, but atypical only in ferocity. Most note users would rather fight than switch.

I'll reveal how to overcome this irrational fear very soon. For now, please understand that I wean students away from notes to *ad-lib* not because I'm a sadist, but because in today's fast-paced world the latter is the only method that has a fighting chance of holding attention.

Ad-Lib—The Certified Winner

What an *ad-lib* really is requires careful definition. It does not mean speaking extemporaneously. To the contrary, spontaneity in public communication is devastating over the long run. You may get away with it on certain occasions, but measured against a number of appearances, it will fail on a ratio of about eight to one. There are just too many variables.

What *ad-lib* means to me is that although the audience perceives an impromptu presentation, in reality the message has been prepared so carefully that not only the material is committed to mind, but also the facial expressions, vocal nuances, and body language that accompany it.

I deliberately use the words *committed to mind* instead of memory. A presentation should *never* be fully memorized. Attempting to speak as if programmed is way too risky. Forget one sentence and the entire speech is out of kilter. Blank out on the next section you plan to cover and the lapse causes a terrible anxiety. By contrast, "committed to mind" means that only the key headings of the material have been memorized. The actual language you use in the speech can vary depending upon the mood of the moment.

I can illustrate both the difference between the two and the technique required to *ad-lib* best by describing the way I prepare for a public presentation. As I pointed out earlier, we almost always speak about subjects we are comfortable with and knowledgeable about. I am never asked to discuss the burgeoning field of genetics or how to grow crops on arid land. I speak about communications. It is my business and my area of expertise. Again, these same restrictions apply to you regardless of trade or profession.

In analyzing the various themes and aspects of my profession, it is easy to separate them into self-contained units or building blocks. For example, look at this book's table of contents. It represents capsules of expertise that I have thought about over the years and have shaped into easily deliverable form. Mention stage fright to me and I can pour out a great amount of information on the subject. Ask about tricks in controlling an audience and I will expound at length about *that*. Why not? I have lived with those issues most of my adult life. The significance of this familiarity with my material is enormous. When called upon to speak, I do not have to worry about what I am going to say. I have only to select the topics for the particular appearance and the order in which I am going to discuss them. I do not have to memorize their content, only the three or four headings necessary to remind me of material I have chosen.

Now *ad-libbing* becomes easy. For one audience, I may choose capsules X, C, and Y, for another, capsules D, F, and G. Thereafter, all I am required to do is create an opening to the speech that is tailored to the specific gathering I am addressing and some transition lines to hold my capsules together.

So, to become an *ad-libber*, divide your own subject material into capsules of about five to seven minutes in length. Work hard on getting those capsules into first-rate form. File them away. When called upon to address an audience, simply choose the appropriate capsules, polish them, and deliver them at will. The listeners will believe it is all impromptu. Only you will know differently.

Other Tips

Always increase your supply of capsules. Introduce new ones to listeners only within the framework of other already successful speeches. That way you assure that if the untried capsule is weak or doesn't work, the surefire routines will guarantee the whole speech is not ruined.

Discard capsules that no longer work. The passage of time or a change of events dates certain ideas we once espoused. Too often we hang onto material that no longer makes sense. Go through your collection of capsules every so often and file them in the wastebasket.

Don't worry about saying the same things in the same words over and over. As long as the audience hasn't already heard your gems, your capsules are brand new to them. Only amateurs tend to feel intellectually dishonest repeating concepts or anecdotes.

Yet until your capsules have been repeated dozens of times, they are probably not honed to finest detail. You must create the illusion that the material is fresh and original, but it does not have to be, nor should it be.

Triumphing Over Notes

We return now, as promised, to the philosophical foundation that I hope will enable you to dispense with *notes,* and hold front and center stage cloaked in the sturdier armor of your own wit and resources.

Recall that the two main justifications expressed by people for relying on *notes* are that they protect them against the terrors of blanking out while in front of an audience and help to assure that all important points are covered. Let's examine the last point first.

It is true that an outline helps keep a speaker on track. If an address is visualized as a twenty-minute totality, then remembering point after point for that length of time is difficult. But under my system, you never attempt such a task. Instead, you construct the speech in four five-minute linked capsules. Since the content of each prepared capsule is cohesive, there is really little opportunity to forget or omit elements. All that has to be memorized are the four outline headings of your major segments. And that should not be too difficult for an adult.

As a child, you may have played the game, good for whiling away minutes on a tedious auto trip, called "Going to the Store." It consists of having to recall words alphabetically. The first participant begins by saying, "I went to the store and purchased asparagus." The next continues, "I went to the store and purchased asparagus and Beechnut gum." The third chimes in, "I went to the store and bought asparagus, Beechnut gum, and cantaloupes." And so on. Victory is determined by who can recite the longest list without getting lost. My eleven-year-old daughter, Jennifer, has hung in there for as many as thirty-five words, the entire alphabet plus nine letters on a second go-around. If a sixth-grader can do that, I find it hard to believe some of my clients who actually plead inability to commit a few outline headings to memory. But I simply refuse to let them get away with it, any more than I sympathize with protests from you, my reader.

But suppose you do forget a capsule, skipping as it were from "A" to "C" by mistake. So what? Almost without fail, the lost segment pops into mind before you finish. Since it is self-contained by design, you always can insert it with a line like, "One of the things I meant to cover was . . ." No harm done at all.

To lay this concern to final rest, let's hypothesize the worst: The forgotten capsule remains forgotten and is never aired. Again, so what? Few points are of such importance in oral communication that if you fail to make them, the earth stops spinning on its axis. Indeed, a forgotten bit of material usually is the least important part of your message or it would not have been misplaced so easily.

You insist that every point you plan to make is vital and has to be included. Okay, then I yield. The concepts I provide here are meant to guide, not be absolute dicta that must be followed under any circumstance. When every word counts, use text or notes and be happy. Just don't fall into that trap unnecessarily, since much of the value of your presentation will be measured by the image you create, not the syllables you orate. An *ad-lib* presentation enhances one's image.

Now, what about blanking out entirely? Fear strikes, the mind empties like a sieve, the speaker stands naked before the roaring mob, robbed of all dignity and protection. I agree that it is not a pleasant feeling when thirty or three hundred faces are staring up at you, waiting for a next word that fails to come. But here is the clincher. How does that audience *know* you are lost unless you tell them?

One of the unshakable myths believed by amateur communicators is that, while making a public appearance, they develop a windowpane in their foreheads that enables viewers to know exactly what they are thinking. Where did this fantasy come from? Audiences know only what they are told or shown. If a speaker, when lost, falters, breaks into a raging sweat, or begins to offer apologies for the lapse, then the secret is out and a most uncomfortable moment exists for all concerned. But if the presenter bluffs, stalls, and fakes his way for only fifteen or twenty seconds of dead time, the clouds clear and a pathway emerges that saves the day.

How to perform this illusion? Here's a trick I use when momentarily numbed. I take a long pause, screw up my face and look to the ceiling as if a great idea is forming in my head. After all, since the perception is that I am speaking off-the-cuff anyhow, I'm entitled to show thought in action. Then, with great confidence, I begin to utter something meaningless: "As I thought of what I wanted to say to you here today, so many ideas went through my head, so many concepts were important, that I found it hard to select those most essential. This is a complex field, but it seemed to me that for you, the most relevant things to keep in mind had to do with . . ." And on and on and on, until one of my capsules jumps into focus. It always does.

I learned this method of vamping until ready while doing a daily hour-long television show in Baltimore. The program aired at 9:00 A.M. *Live.* As with anything else, some mornings were more *live* than others.

One morning, I began to question a guest, and got into the middle of the thought and suddenly realized I had gone totally blank. I didn't recall how I had begun the statement or where in the world it was heading. Horribly unsettled, I blew the whole affair. Acknowledging I was lost, I admitted to being out of control and made a total ass of myself in the process.

With experience I learned to bluff my way through such lapses. I would ramble for ten seconds or so and finally pick up the strands of an idea that got me off the hook. No one ever knew the difference. To repeat: Words disappear as spoken. No one who has heard them has the power to look back and realize how empty your words were. Audiences only know what you tell and show them at that instant.

I promise that if you go through this experience, getting lost and recovering without ever revealing your true state, the fear of finding yourself in such a situation will never be a bother again. And you will have managed to make the transition from *notes* to *ad-lib,* a move that will radically improve your skills as a communicator.

Plan in advance methods for handling a crisis that may develop during a public appearance. Regardless of the approach you decide upon, the key is to never let anyone watching conclude that you ever had a crisis or moment of doubt.

16 Readiness Is All

Let's return now to the other offstage activities required of you before an appearance.

No matter what method of delivery you choose, it must be practiced extensively before curtain time. Practice does not mean just thinking through what you will say. Practice means saying it —*aloud*—again and again. There is a huge gap between thoughts securely locked in your mind and thoughts you articulate. If you wish quick, ample proof of this, stop right now and describe what your occupation consists of in thirty seconds. Unless you are unusually glib, you will be shocked at how difficult it is to precisely describe the way you make your living, a topic you're obviously familiar with.

Ironically, high-ranking executives are particularly prone to inadequate practice because of their opportunity to delegate responsibility. Able to tap multiple resources, the executive orders the services of a staff speechwriter. The writer is summoned, told in bold outlines the issues the boss wishes to address and the date a first draft has to be submitted. The draft arrives on schedule. The executive edits, makes additions and deletions, and ships the text back to the writer for another try. Often this procedure is repeated several times. But, although hours are spent polishing content, the finished version is typically not on paper until a day before the presentation is to be given. Inevitably, the executive practices his delivery by silently mouthing the words while he enjoys a drink on the airplane that takes him to his speaking engagement. In spite of his good intentions, the actual presentation turns out to be a dud. Simply put, he didn't do enough practicing.

To practice, you must use a recorder. Video is preferable, but audio will suffice. If only the latter is available, stand in front of a mirror for visual feedback. If you have access to video, set up the camera, aim it at yourself, and start talking. Study your image on the playback monitor carefully. Is your face animated enough? Does your voice have life and color? Are your body movements studied or jerky? How is the overall pacing? The most important question in this phase of our discussion is: Does the material work? Does it meet all the standards of direction and coherence discussed in the preceding chapters?

If you study yourself objectively, the screen or the mirror and audio recorder will provide the answers. It is essential to have a recording device because that image and sound is the *you* the audience sees. Add improvements to and eliminate flaws from your delivery to make sure it is a reflection you are proud of. To refresh your recollection about techniques for accomplishing this, see Chapter 8.

Adding Visuals

Visuals, or audiovisuals as they are commonly called, can do much for a presentation if they are properly utilized. We should first define the term.

When you stand in front of an audience, there is one visual available: *you.* That is what listeners see while you speak. If you are sufficiently dynamic, that can be enough. But if the material being delivered is dry or complex, other visuals may be required. The following are some choices.

Charts

These can consist of placards affixed to the walls around the room or sheets on an easel. Using an easel has the advantage of controlling access to the flow of information until the speaker wishes it revealed. Only one card at a time is on display. The disadvantage is having to fumble around, either turning pages or removing cards to reveal new ones. Wall charts encourage a speaker to use physical movement. So do chalk and magnetic boards.

Chalk or Magnetic Boards

I have seen these props used most effectively, but only by very experienced speakers. It requires a calm, secure touch to turn your back to an audience while deliberately drawing words or juggling magnetic bits.

Slides

This is a common prop, commonly overused. But one advantage of slides is that they handle easily. The speaker controls the clicker and can advance or reverse at will, provided the carousel works properly. Often it doesn't. Be certain, up front, that slides are in the appropriate order and that a substitute bulb is available if the main one should blow. Take nothing for granted.

Transparencies

I have a prejudice against transparencies, also referred to as viewfoils or overheads. To me, they are the most boring way to provide visual information. The print usually comes straight from a typewriter with little variation in style, color, or size to break the monotony. The advantage of overheads is that they can be produced quickly and at little cost. Disadvantages, other than drabness, are that they have to be handled manually, placed and replaced on the projection machine one by one. A presentation can become ludicrous and embarrassing when a speaker continually fumbles with the focus mechanism or stoops over to pick up transparencies that slipped from grasp and floated to the floor.

Videotape or Film

These two visual elements differ both in flavor and utilization. Film offers a soft, almost poetic feeling and clearly represents the past. It is most appropriate and effective when you are trying to create a particular mood or sense of perspective. It is less successful in conveying hard information. Running the film can be cumbersome. The 16-mm projector must be placed in the middle of the audience, front and central to the screen. Easy access by the speaker to attendees is thus blocked off for all practical purposes. Furthermore, the room must be darkened to enhance visibility, and the whirring of the machinery can be distracting.

Videotape creates an illusion of *now*. It is direct and gives a dramatic sense of immediacy. Freeze-framing, at the speaker's choice, permits a particular image to remain on view almost indefinitely. Modern recorders are lightweight (nine pounds or even less), and a single cord connected to a receiver is all that's required for picture and sound. Since most of us are comfortable receiving information from a TV screen, videotape is a familiar, and effective way of sending it.

Here are some caveats that apply to use of any type of visual. Unfortunately, they are more often ignored than observed.

Don't Overuse Them!

Visuals are meant to supplement a speaker's performance, not substitute for it. Slides, as I hinted above, are most subject to abuse. I have watched presentations that are backed by these pictures from the opening word to the last. That is an absolutely dreadful approach. Here's a story that illustrates the point.

I was called in to work with a corporate president who was scheduled to deliver a major address to an economics association. On his first run-through for me, the executive strode to the lectern, began with a salutation, the lights dimmed, pictures filled the screen behind him, and the formal speech began. It continued for twenty minutes, with every single phrase backed by a slide. Before the last paragraph, the lights were turned back up, the executive expressed his appreciation for the opportunity to address the audience, and the performance was over.

The client looked at me and said, "Well?"

"It's wonderful," I responded, "except for one small problem. Why don't we just put a tape recorder on the lectern and let it roll with your message? Since no one will ever see you, why waste your time being there?"

Visuals do help reinforce the audio message, but they also demand listeners make a choice. Do they watch the prop or the speaker? What the speaker says tends to fade away when there are endless pictures to stare at. Much of what is said is forever lost.

My premise is that the speaker is the star, the featured event the audience figuratively or literally has paid to see. There is a famous quote attributed to the legendary Hollywood producer Sam Goldwyn about why he never made films with strong underlying themes. "If I want to send a message," says Goldwyn, "I go to Western Union." A variation on this is: "If I want to look at pictures, I go to the museum." Speeches should spotlight speakers, and what they have to say; they should never be overwhelmed by visuals and other props.

In using visuals, be sure to restrict them to material so complicated or so important that it deserves graphic support. To do otherwise is to diminish the importance of your message and *you*.

Use Visuals in Blocks!

It is distracting to show two pictures and then speak, show another one and speak some more, and so on. It is far better to speak without visuals for a period, show a minute or two of pictures, then speak again before showing another block. In the beginning of this section, I urged you to treat a speech as a produced public appearance. If you attend a musical comedy, you will note that dialogue is followed by a production number that may be followed by more dialogue and then a quiet ballad. Vary your visual props the same way so they are neither jumpy nor monotonous.

Don't Talk to the Visuals

Many amateurs find, in using a slide screen or flip chart, a golden opportunity to avoid looking at the faces in the crowd. Of course, the back of the speaker's head does very little communicating. The proper approach is to glance at, or point to, the particular visual being utilized, and then turn back to the audience while discussing it. Another good practice is to pause after highlighting visual information, giving listeners a chance to digest it. Then regain and hold attention with the oral presentation.

Make Sure Visuals Can Be Seen!

Think of how often you hear a speaker introduce a slide or drawing with these words: "You may not be able to see this but . . ." If graphics are not clear and large enough to be seen easily in the last row, don't use them. Instead of enlightenment, there will be confusion and a negative reaction to your presentation. For best results, limit information on any single image. Illustrations are helpful. If words are the medium, employ a clear typeface and both capital and small letters. Five to six words per line are plenty. Severely limit the number of lines. Simple, strong words and short sentences are a must.

Make Them Pretty!

Aesthetically gratifying stimuli provide more information. So make appropriate use of color contrast. White, yellow, or red letters and pictures should be set off against a background of black, dark blue, or brown. If because of time or budget constraints, meeting these standards is impossible, at least make certain that hand-drawn charts or viewfoils are neat and clear.

Before moving on to the techniques of capturing and controlling an audience, let's summarize the ingredients that make up a successful presentation. The Public Appearance Checklist that follows can be utilized whenever you have to be in the spotlight.

Public Appearance Checklist

I. **Material**

    a. Does your speech make the points you wish to cover?

    b. Does your language communicate?

        1. Is it bold and colorful?

        2. Is it free of professional terminology or jargon?

        3. Is it expressed in the fewest words possible to make point?

    c. Are the beginning and finish powerful?

    d. Is your content full of "gee whizzes"?

    e. Is total length within twenty-minute range?

II. **Delivery**

    a. Script

        1. Are you certain you need it?

        2. Is it typed in capitals with wide margins?

    b. Ad-lib

        1. Have you prepared content in building blocks?

        2. Are back-up blocks available if necessary?

III. **Audiovisual Supports**

    a. Do you really need them?

    b. Have you chosen the best mode for the situation?

    c. Have you rehearsed using them?

    d. Are they colorful and legible?

IV. **PRACTICE! PRACTICE! PRACTICE!** using a video recorder or an audio recorder while standing in front of a mirror. Get a sense of how you *look* making a speech and it will help you look good when you are up there actually doing it.

17 Capturing and Controlling an Audience

What would we see if we possessed X-ray vision and could penetrate the minds of people sitting in a convention audience? Let's speculate.

The sharply dressed guy in the third row, with the striped shirt and paisley bow tie, is thinking fondly of last night's romantic dalliance with the red-headed stunner seated near the back. She is pondering the affair, too, only less fondly. In the middle of the group is a matronly lady in a business suit, worrying about her daughter away at college. The preppy-looking fellow nine rows back, fifth seat in from the aisle, is concerned about his left knee, still aching from a seven-mile run on Sunday.

Audiences are composed of individuals, each with their joys and problems. When the opportunity exists, the mind will push these personal preoccupations front and center, blocking out the sight and sound of the event taking place on stage.

Without needing X-ray vision, an observant speaker quickly picks up signals of inattentive listeners. The audience's behavior tells crystal-clear tales. The Romeo with the paisley tie is staring blankly out the window. His last-night's love is studying her finger-nails. The harassed mom is doodling on her notepad. And the weekend athlete is distractedly rubbing that tender kneecap.

So what, you may wonder? If a certain percentage of an audience wants to engage in reveries, why not let them? The answer lies in a fundamental equation of group dynamics.

$$\text{Individual Inattention} = \text{Group Disarray}$$

Allow one individual to stargaze and ten copycats will do the same. A doodler encourages others to become amateur Picassos. A finger snapper or foot tapper will provoke a small chorus of accompaniment. The phenomenon is much the same as that which occurs at a stage play when one person in the audience starts to cough. Within minutes of the first burst, a cacophony develops. As social animals, we are prone to mimicry.

It's difficult if not impossible to communicate when an audience is doing its own thing. So capturing and controlling a group is essential to getting a message across. The process begins long before the actual appearance takes place. And it requires *selfish-ness*—a trait of which we are normally ashamed. But think of it as selfishness in a good cause. Experience teaches professional communicators that accommodating the needs of the support staff and others, when facing an audience, is a sure way of losing sight of their own main goal—*to be a successful crowd pleaser.* Let me explain what I mean by that.

Setting the Stage

You have followed all the proper procedures in preparing for your appearance. Your material is substantive, scintillating, and solidly structured. You have practiced your delivery until it is down cold. Effective visuals and props have been added where needed. Are you finished? *No!*

There is another component to a successful presentation: setting the stage properly. Here is a typical scenario:

A trade society calls, requesting you to be the keynote speaker at its annual banquet. Your reputation and expertise has attracted them. The opportunity sounds challenging and you accept. Terms are agreed upon. Date, place, time, and honorarium (if any) are confirmed in a letter.

At the appointed hour, you arrive and find that the audience is twice as large as you anticipated, and the room has no amplification system. The lectern is placed directly in front of an undraped window, shadowing the podium area with back light. You expected the group to consist of middle-aged businessmen. But women are present and the average age is sixty and upward. Your subject matter is no longer applicable. Now what do you do? You know you'll "die" before you open your mouth. And you deserve to. Why? Because you avoided your responsibility to make a preappearance investigation.

When you commit to a speaking engagement, learn as much in advance as possible about audience and environment. Don't settle for superficial answers from the program leader. Press for details. Arrive at the location an hour or so in advance. Size up the room. If there are undraped windows, see if they can be covered. Attendees won't look at you when they have an attractive outside view to distract them. Fuss with the seating arrangement. Too many chairs for the size of the group signal that people will spread throughout the area available, filling in the back rows and leaving the front ones empty. Cluster people tightly together. It establishes group cohesion, beneficial to both crowd control and positive reaction. It is not by accident that restaurants seat patrons, one section at a time, until the entire place is occupied.

Check on the temperature. If the room is warm before the group is seated, imagine how steamy it will become once bodies are in place. Too much heat is an invitation to sleep. Chill the room down as much as possible and then turn the air conditioner off when it's time for your speech. The drone of a wheezing machine can drown nuances of delivery.

If you plan to use a microphone, check it out. Different voice resonances call for different volume levels. The wrong one for your voice can be crippling. Make sure there is a long microphone cord so you can stroll into the audience, if you decide to do so. Practice removing the mike from the clip and replacing it. Struggling clumsily with the instrument in front of fifty people is always good for the kind of laughs you don't want or need.

All these alterations are, of course, subject to the reality of what is possible, given the circumstances. Fixed seating is fixed seating and you have to live with it. A bad sound system can't be made good by willing it so. But make what changes you can to maximize your presentation. That's just good sense.

Doing It Your Own Way

Length of Talk

The chairperson says, "We would like your address to last about forty-five minutes." Knowing that forty-five minutes is too long, you politely demur, suggesting your presentation run half that length. The chairperson is unrelenting: "You don't understand my problem. We have you scheduled for 11:15 A.M. Lunch doesn't begin until shortly after noon. If you speak only twenty minutes, there will be a horde of people wandering around aimlessly for nearly half an hour. Perhaps you might bring along extra slides— or build in more of a question-and-answer period."

An amateur speaker begins to yield at this point. How can such a good-faith plea be resisted? Easily. To be successful—*be selfish!* Say this: "I will be happy to fill the forty-five minutes of time for you." But when the moment of reckoning comes, do twenty minutes and sit down. There will be no complaint from the group. Orators who ramble on endlessly are resented; few listeners ever protest that the speaker sat down too soon.

In the same way, fight off the chairperson who wants to trim your remarks on site. It happens this way. Introductory comments run way too long. Worried about the caterer's ire over a delayed lunch or dinner, the chairperson whispers in your ear, "We are running a bit behind schedule. Can you cut it down?"

Amateurs will attempt to rush through an already tightly structured presentation in ten minutes or cut the heart out of its substance. Professionals will say, "Certainly," and then present their routine exactly the way they prepared it.

Subject Matter

The presentation that works is an *illusion*—appearing spontaneous but actually carefully prepared, polished, and recycled as often as possible. Beware then the host who tries to tell you what to talk about. The dialogue goes like this: "You're going to speak about communications, Mr. Zenker. Wonderful. What would really be of interest to our people is an analysis of the history of the First Amendment, with special emphasis on the case of *Roe v. Doe.*"

From my point of view, there is one slight difficulty. I know little of the history of the First Amendment and absolutely nothing about *Roe* v. *Doe.* So I say, "Sorry, I have little experience or knowledge in that area of communications."

"But Mr. Zenker," comes the rejoinder, "I am certain if you do a little research . . ."

Yield and be doomed to a poor presentation. To meet the needs of the host, you will discard a presentation package that you know is a winner and try to create a new one on short notice. That's insanity. Instead, promise him anything. But when the spotlight shines, fall back into material you are comfortable with. If you handle it properly, no one will notice the dodge. Using my First Amendment example: "Rights under the First Amendment today are quite different from those envisioned by our Founding Fathers. A series of Supreme Court interpretations have shaped it into a strong force for political discussion in some cases and limited its uses severely in others. What interests me most is . . ."

And then segue into your own material. In my experience, few members of an audience know or care what the topic is. Their only interest is whether the speech is rewarding.

Will Such Control Tactics Be Perceived as Offensive?

A reasonable question from you is: "How will my host react to such apparent arrogance on my part? Will I be judged harshly as uncooperative and untrustworthy?"

The answer depends upon your degree of *savior faire* in controlling demands made upon you. If you are smooth enough to tactfully reduce the chairperson's requirements for the length of your speech from forty-five to thirty minutes in the first example, you can trim another five to seven minutes during the actual engagement without anyone even noticing it. Similarly, when you agree to shorten your speech because the program is behind schedule, only you will ever know that you ran it exactly the prepared length. As to choice of topic, I deliberately provided a highly exaggerated illustration of manipulativeness. In most cases, you and your host will find an acceptable middle ground because it is in your mutual interest to do so. In other words, there is little reason for you to come across as intentionally rude while exercising your control tactics.

Even if you should have to blatantly assert your rights, you will find that all will be forgiven if your presentation is well received. The chairperson, basking in the glow of your success, will quickly forget your "selfishness."

In another era, when Jack Paar hosted the "Tonight Show," he and Ed Sullivan engaged in a well-publicized feud over fees paid to performing talent. Sullivan paid huge salaries to the stars who appeared on his program, whereas "Tonight Show" policy enabled Paar to obtain their services for union scale. Infuriated by the difference in compensation Sullivan announced that no actor or singer who worked for a minimum wage on the "Tonight Show" would ever be welcome again on his stage. I remember a cynical columnist translating that pronouncement for those who didn't understand the realities of show business. "What Sullivan means," he wrote, "is that he never will use any of those SOB's again— *unless he needs them.*" In a like manner, if your own act is successful enough, your prickliness backstage will be overlooked.

Time of Appearance

An audience's energy level surges and ebbs like the tide. Early in the morning, it is at midlevel. Some attendees, the larks, are up and raring to go. Others, the owls, are barely conscious. They drink cup after cup of caffeine just to start the blood flowing.

Midmorning finds the group on a steady keel. This heightened attention level lasts right up to lunch, unless it is served unusually late.

For many people, after lunch, expecially if alcoholic beverages were consumed, it is nap time. We have never built afternoon siestas into our life style, but people take them just the same, often with their eyes wide open.

By midafternoon, hormones are pumping away and again the audience is alive and willing to participate.

After 4:00 P.M., there are just two things on a group's unannounced agenda—the bar or the airport.

I could continue with this daily log, but you get the idea. The time of day you speak can have a major effect on how successful the presentation turns out to be. Analyze the overall pacing of the program, then jockey for the best position.

Order of Appearance

I worked a convention once where Art Buchwald was the main event. The satirist is an amusing speaker with a wealth of good material as entertaining as his columns. Luckily, my presentation preceded his. Had it followed, I would have been dead in the water. His conclusion consisted of a patriotic paean to America. The audience took a full ten minutes to settle down after their enthusiastic response to his talk.

Try to learn who else will be on the program. If superstars are appearing, make certain your own slot is once or twice removed from theirs.

These tactics do not signify arrogance or ego on your part. They are your survival skills. Sometimes, though, there is no opportunity to activate them. If the boss says you will speak after lunch about a tedious topic for forty-five minutes, then I guess that's your fate. But if there is room to maneuver, then as a *professional communicator,* for heaven's sake—and yours—maneuver.

On-Site Control Techniques

In spite of your best efforts, there will be occasions when you look out at a group and see a crowd of doodlers, chatterbugs, and catatonics. What do you do? As I indicated initially, rude behavior by one or two individuals can infect the entire audience like a virus. Take curative action immediately.

Switch Subject Matter.

The nice part of constructing speeches in building-block form is that it provides flexibility. Although you may have expected to talk about themes "A", "F," and "X," move to blocks "B," "T," and "Z" as an alternative if your first choice is failing.

Break for Questions.

No biblical admonition requires you take questions at the end of the presentation only. Pause for some give-and-take until the level of audience participation increases.

Physically Challenge Those Who Are Inattentive.

I stressed earlier that the curse of speaking from text or notes is that you are locked behind the lectern. By contrast, "prepared ad-lib" frees you to stride directly into the midst of the masses and intimidate the inattentive among them. Lean in on a private conversation; confront doodlers with a fixed stare or quick question. Adults are like children. They dread being singled out from the group. Challenge their lack of attention and watch everyone sit up straight, hoping you will direct your attentions elsewhere.

The Cantankerous Audience

Working as I do with industries and companies under public fire, I am often asked what methods are available for handling a fiercely angry audience. Using your instinct, based on your experience, helps a great deal. The communicator who is able to deftly turn a hostile crowd into a more harmonious one is seasoned enough to understand the factors at work in the particular situation because he or she has faced similar occasions many times in the past.

Here are some of the negative experiences that can turn an audience hostile.

Long Delays

A group that has been waiting for a program to start can become irritable by the time it does.

Disappointment

When the food has been rotten, the service intolerable, the room is sweltering, and the acoustics are nonexistent, the speaker is a natural target for the victims' wrath.

Bias

In the late 1970s, New York's Office of Mental Retardation and Developmental Disability decided to open community homes for its clients. Staffers from the department consistently faced gatherings of neighborhood residents who were furious about this invasion of "insane misfits." The bias, fundamentally incorrect though it was, had to be acknowledged by the speaker.

I saw another example of the destructive impact of bias while conducting a workshop in Toronto for the Canadian members of a United States trade association. All of the speakers who preceded me had carelessly offered material more appropriate for a U. S. audience, overlooking the national sensitivity of Canadians about their powerful cousin to the south. Practically before I opened my mouth, irate members of the audience were ready to attack me.

What to Do?

Up to a Point, Let the Anger Vent

Given an opportunity to air their gripes, people usually settle down. Never try to squelch the eruption in an autocratic manner.

To the Extent Possible, Disassociate Yourself from the Causes of the Audience's Irritation

I didn't cook the food or build the hotel or cause the delay. I noted to the Canadian group that I didn't work for the association nor did I book the other guests on the program. I bore responsibility only for my segment, which I promised would be pertinent since communication utilizes the same skills whether practiced north or south of the border.

Call an Intermission

It may not have been scheduled, but if a three-minute standing pause would do wonders for everyone's mood, take the break.

Keep Cool

Your manner at the lectern, in an emotionally charged environment, must be objective and patient. Never attempt to lead questioners with expressions like "you agree, don't you?" or "I am sure you understand why." Resentment and resistance will result. Try to stay away from using inflammatory language such as "that is ignorant . . . or impossible . . . or superficial." Your demeanor must appear respectful, confident, and open to alternative opinions.

Make an Offering

If you can bring concessions with you, parcel them out like candy. It is not altruism that leads an airline to offer free drinks to passengers who have been delayed for two hours because of a mechanical failure. It's a way of calming their anger and maintaining good public relations.

Sometimes the Bear Gets You

Suppose you pull out all the stops and nothing helps. The angry audience refuses to be mollified; the drowsy one refuses to come alive. Then do ten minutes instead of twenty . . . and quit. Don't try to be superhuman.

In 1978, a trade group in Baltimore signed me to speak at their annual banquet. When I entered the ballroom, I saw my troubles immediately. A thousand people were jammed into a space adequate for six hundred. The head table had been positioned near the kitchen door. Worst of all, the hospitality lounges had been serving drinks for at least two hours.

I tried everything. I had structured a talk of serious intent. Within two minutes after being introduced, I dumped that concept and went to my blocks of straight humor. Somehow, I fought my way out from behind the head table into the seating area. I attempted to physically control anyone in the group looking at me. All to no avail. A constant roar of extraneous chatter made me feel I was lecturing to the Atlantic Ocean.

The association had paid me handsomely for a thirty-minute address. I did eighteen minutes, stuffed the check securely into my pocket, and left for the airport. I've been at this business too long to think I can win them all. When the chemistry is dead set against you, pack up your bags and seek the safety of home. Sometimes you get the bear; sometimes the bear gets you. There is always another chance down the road.

18 And in Conclusion...

On reviewing my advice to you, I note that I have offered dozens of different dictums. Lists of "dos" and "don'ts" fill the pages. Perhaps this is because, on the printed page, equivocation seems counterproductive. Only mandates manage to endow information with a sense of urgency.

Still, my underlying philosophy remains unshaken. I hope you absorb and make good use of the doctrines offered here, but I also hope you filter them through your own good sense in the process. As the label reads on any powerful medicine: HANDLE WITH CAUTION!

To illustrate: Twenty minutes is an ideal length for the average speech. But in a corporate environment, especially, that time frame may be a dream. When the Committee of Finance demands you structure an hour-long budget presentation, you can't say "but Arnold Zenker suggests a twenty-minute maximum." What I am really saying is a full-hour presentation requires enormous production effort. You might consider beginning with a seven-minute monologue, switch to three minutes of slides, break for question-

and-answer interaction, return to wall charts, and then do another monologue. But please recognize the need to do more than just "talk" the entire period.

In the same vein, I curse the use of *notes* as an unnecessary crutch and urge you adopt an *ad-lib* approach. But if your material contains numerous statistics or specific quotations, of course you may use notes to help you recall them. Just don't fall back upon total reliance on notes as the easy way of getting through an appearance. It may be easy; it won't be successful.

Think! Think! Think! Treat a public appearance as you would a problem in your own business. Analyze the issue, determine the desired goal, and then with calculation structure those components that will help assure success.

Develop a Style of Your Own

Many years ago, a public-relations firm representing Frank Perdue (the chicken tycoon) asked me to anonymously evaluate his speaking style at a marketing conference. In spite of Perdue's success as a television-commercial pitchman, the firm had questions about his effectiveness at the lectern. They need not have worried. Technically, Perdue's delivery required refinement. He tended to speak too softly, rambled on too long, and paced the floor in an aimless fashion. Nevertheless, I thought Perdue was sensational. To me, he managed to convey the image of an eastern shore Maryland farmer who slept in the coop just to guarantee good quality. I left the session ready to fork out an extra dime a pound for his brand of poultry. Perdue's sense of style—his authenticity—overcame his deficiencies.

Young people rarely possess a unique style. It takes maturity and experience to learn who we really are or want to be. But I cringe when I observe older folks with a still undeveloped personal style. Blandness is so boring. A person forty or older should convey a definable *image*. It can be crusty, jolly, intellectual, aggressive, dour, or humorous—just so long as it is stimulating and interesting. If you haven't yet done so, begin to develop your own persona, one appropriate to your current age.

Pressing the Ego Button

I love appearing before audiences. When I'm on top of my game, the feeling is akin to what a gambler experiences on a high roll. Everything works out exactly the way it should. Laughter bursts out on schedule, tension is triggered at the proper time. And heartfelt, vigorous applause is a tangible tribute to my victory.

I even love appearing before audiences when I fail. The experience is fascinating. Why did it go sour? Where did I lose them? To me, a chess match is tame by comparison.

I find it incredible that so many people shy away from the pure fun and instant gratification enjoyed by the communicator of professional caliber. A nuclear engineer can labor for ten years before the product of his or her skill and efforts finally goes on line. A salesperson can wait months to learn if planning and preparation resulted in a booked order. Progress is time consuming.

But when that same engineer or salesperson walks on stage, there is the giddy anticipation of instant feedback—of knowing the jury will reach a verdict in twenty minutes. If the outcome is positive, high spirits last all day. If it's thumbs down . . . ? Note your mistakes and vow never to repeat them again.

But remember this! Because professional communicators know their craft, the outcome is going to be triumphant 95 percent of the time. It has to be. They planned it that way. So 95 percent of the time, the speaking engagement or TV experience is a marvelous trip.

Why do you think the Bob Hopes and George Burnses are still at it in their eighties? Certainly not for the financial reward. Neither man could spend his accumulated wealth in the years remaining to them. No! They keep trotting onto center stage because few other endeavors in life offer the heady rush of experiencing an audience that loves you.

Don't think of a public appearance as a burden. Think of it as an opportunity to play master puppeteer—with the audience dangling at the end of your words. Move them. Make them pensive, make them patriotic. The power is yours, and what a wonderful power it is.

What I say to my clients, who are bright, accomplished people, I now say to you:

"You take enormous pride in performing your own job well. How can you be satisfied being perceived as mediocre when appearing in a public forum? How can you tolerate knowing an audience thought you ho-hum? It doesn't have to be that way if you will put your ego on the line.

"Take risks. Draft punchy material. Throw away crutches. Venture attempts at humor. Be manipulative if it helps you become masterful. Aim to be a *star—a crowd pleaser.* Your very determination to shine will assure that you do."

Index